NEW DAD

THE ULTIMATE PREGNANCY GUIDE FOR FIRST-TIME
DADS [INCLUDES WEEK BY WEEK PREGNANCY
DEVELOPMENT AND TIPS ON HOW TO PREPARE,
WHAT TO EXPECT FROM CONCEPTION TO BIRTH]

RYAN ERICKSON

CONTENTS

FREE GIFT
JUST FOR YOU!

From this free gift, you can find out:

7 mistakes first-time dads make and actionable tips you can apply immediately.

Just visit the link www.ryanericksonbooks.com

INTRODUCTION

I sat there with my mouth wide open, but I couldn't breathe. It felt like someone had just locked up all the oxygen. My skin turned pale. I was panicking, and it was hard to hide it from my wife. She had that worried look on her face, staring at me as if I were just about to do something stupid (like run away from home). She calmly sat me down at the kitchen table, patted my back, and asked if I would be okay. The newborn started screaming through the monitor—again!

"Am I going to be okay?" I must have said aloud. Between the screams coming from the monitor and my anxiety, I felt a bit disoriented. Was this fear I was feeling? But shouldn't I have been happier? Wasn't it a good thing? what happened? Married couples are supposed to celebrate when they get baby news, right? Babies are a blessing to a new family and all that hoopla. At least, that's what others said. I didn't actually know. I wasn't sure what to think or how to feel.

My wife gently held my hand and pressed it tightly against her chest, reassuring me that we were all going to be okay. At the time, I struggled to believe that statement.

I'm a smart, hard-working man, a loving husband, and, by most accounts, pretty successful at what I do. But somehow, standing there that morning, after receiving the news that we were pregnant for the second time only nine months after our first baby, I didn't feel smart or successful at all. The truth is, I felt very lost.

I was struggling tremendously with the changes brought by the first baby. Now she was telling me about baby number two? The past year had been like a mash-up of a horror movie, a zombie apocalypse, and a poorly scripted D.C. movie. Thinking that another baby was on the way was a bit too much, even for a mentally stable guy like me.

Now, I know what you're thinking. Isn't this book about being a first-time dad? You're right; it is. But the guy sharing this journey with you is someone who didn't realize how messy and stressful being a dad can be until it was too late. Here's a guy (me) who thought all I needed to do was show up for the prenatal visits, maybe massage my wife's feet once in a while and stay out of her way when she was in her moods, then go out there and provide for my family—like a real man should.

If you've been listening to that kind of talk, it's time to discard that crap. Becoming a great husband and a great dad takes a lot more preparation, knowledge, and personal growth than most men realize. Some of us don't actually get it until we're too deep in the game. Only then do we start realizing how much of a screw-up we are, and sometimes, we end up having melt-downs like the one I had that morning after learning of baby number two. I reacted like a teenager who wanted out. Trust me, fellas, that is the last thing your wife needs, especially when she's going through her own roller coaster.

So, if you're currently caught in a situation where you're feeling lost, unprepared, anxious, alone, distraught, and mentally exhausted, I feel you, brother. I've been there. It took me baby number two to realize that I needed to get my sh** together and become a great father and husband. By the time we hit baby number three, my pregnancy and post-delivery experience was way more enjoyable than the first two trials. I'm not saying it was easy—being a dad is never easy—

but it was enjoyable and meaningful for both my Mrs. and me. And looking back, I wish I'd come across material like this so that I could have nailed it the first time around. That's why I'm thrilled that you got your hands on this book. Regardless of your reasons for grabbing a copy, this book is sure to open your eyes to a different approach to fatherhood and guide you as you evolve and become the man your family needs and loves.

I kid you not, Ray Romano wasn't half lying when he said that having children is like living in a frat house—nobody sleeps, everything's broken, and there's a lot of throwing up. It sounds awful, and yes, some days, it does feel overwhelming. But it's also one of the most fulfilling gigs you will ever have. Sure, you'll get to a point where taking a nap feels more desirable than going out to a romantic dinner with your wife, but once you catch on to the big picture and the fulfilling purpose that dadhood brings, every obstacle, sleepless night, and even the vomits will feel 100% worth it.

WHAT YOU CAN EXPECT FROM THIS BOOK:

Now, I know you already have a boatload of questions. You're probably wondering, will everything be centered around the baby now? What will happen to our intimacy? What happens if my wife has to quit her job to stay home, and how will that impact my finances? Can I still buy the new Xbox, or does that make me a moron now that I have bigger expenses to deal with? Will I even have time to play with my Xbox? These are all great questions, and this book will ensure you have all the answers you need to make great decisions as a first-time dad. Let's start with an all-important answer - you're not a moron for wanting to invest $400 on an Xbox, but your wife might think so if you do it now. So maybe, put a pause on that. And you won't have the time or peace of mind anyway to spend hours on video games once the baby arrives unless you go to a friend's house. And no, that's not a good idea when your wife needs you most.

This book combines my experience as a "first-time dad" three times over (because yes, every pregnancy and baby follows its unique path) and my research and study in family counseling. You're going to learn everything you need to know about being a first-time dad, how to lovingly and fully support your partner through pregnancy, what to do after the baby arrives and how to handle your insecurities, anxieties as a man with added responsibilities. We'll cover practical tips and strategies that will reduce the current apprehension you might have whether you're thinking about your finances, your intimacy with your partner during and after the baby, or even your mental well-being. Many guys stress over the unknown, i.e., future complications and challenges of a new family, and some stress over whether or not they have what it takes to be great fathers. I struggled with that quite a bit, so I'll share with you the exact strategies I've used on myself and my clients to heal and prepare for this new role of fatherhood.

Our approach will remain simple. We shall remain true to the perspective that to become the best version of yourself for your family, and you don't need complex or gruesome solutions. You need the right starting point and a strong foundation. That's why being a dad isn't always easy, but it should always be simple.

What is the right starting point? To answer that, we need to take a step back and shift our focus to a critical component of this father-husband-new family dynamic: You.

1

FIRST, REALLY GET TO KNOW YOURSELF... AND YOUR WIFE

I recently came across a bumper sticker that said, if something you're about to do scares you a little, that's a good thing. Maybe there's truth in that. I doubt any great performer, athlete, or artist ever steps on stage without that slight tingling of fear looming around. Well, you're about to embark on the greatest adventure of your life. It's going to last a lifetime and begin the moment you receive the pregnancy news. At that moment, if you're like most dads, you likely experienced a 50-50 mix of excitement and fear. That's a good thing. Becoming a first-time dad is uncharted terrain, and the unknown often causes our brains and bodies to send off fear signals.

Discovering that the clock is ticking creates a sense of urgency that was never there before. You might find yourself pumped up with delight for a few minutes, and then slowly, the gravity of the situation kicks in as you start wondering how this will alter your future goals. How expensive are schools? Do you need to move to a better school district? Won't that cost money? How do you even change a diaper? Will you need to babyproof the entire apartment? What if something goes wrong during labor? How does the birth process even work? Isn't it horrifying, and what if I pass out? Will she ever forgive me? These questions will rush through your mind at various intervals, sometimes keeping you awake all night. I want you to realize that it's normal for you to have this uncomfortable and alarming reaction. It happens to every man who genuinely cares about his wife and starting a family. Stress is expected when you're stretching yourself to this new level. What matters is that you realize that you'll need a total transformation.

FROM DUDE… TO DAD

The version of you that's come this far is not equipped or mature enough to handle the demands of being a full-time dad and family man. Sure, you just fathered a child, but to raise one, you'll need to transform into a modern-day dad. And that's going to require a different mindset, a dadkit jammed with tools and techniques; in short, a total psychological transformation.

Many guys assume that being a dad is some kind of negative sacrifice. I see it as an opportunity to evolve, transform, and unleash a more powerful, purposeful, and responsible version of yourself. If you think about it, that doesn't negatively impact any of your other goals in life. In fact, a better version of you means you get to accomplish bigger and better things. Plenty of research now indicates that dads actually experience hormonal changes in their bodies if they have direct physical interaction with an infant. The more intimate a dad becomes with his baby, the lower his testosterone dips and the more empathetic and soothing he is with his child. Prior to the 1970s, most dads weren't involved with their kids, and there was very little intimate contact during infancy, so it could be why there was a struggle to connect or even experience the real joys of dad hood. Many of us were raised in a household where our father was never home. And even if he was, he was just a few levels down from being a stranger. That affects the kind of father you become if you're not careful. As it turns out, modern-day parenting, especially conscious parenting (which is what you're learning here), can help you experience a connection with your child that makes you not only a better parent but also a better man in society.

Stress and challenges are part of this adventure, but doesn't that apply to every great objective? When you acquire the proper knowledge, skills, and guidance, you can drastically reduce stress and manage the over- whelm that will confront you along the way. That's what I aim to do in this guidebook. Before you start misjudging the contents of this book, let's air out a few things.

This guidebook isn't aimed at helping you with the technical aspects of pregnancy and childbirth. I will be pointing you to the recommended "medical experts" who've already written extensively about the details of each trimester and what you can expect all the way to the child birthing process. You'll have a long list of recommended resources at the end of this book consisting of other books, articles, and videos from authoritative resources and medical practitioners who will provide all the support and clarity you need when it comes to an understanding of what your wife is going through.

However, our primary focus is providing guidance and support for your mental well-being and mindset so you can train your brain to be comfortable with the uncom- fortable. When I became a dad, I noticed that very few books help first-time dads get their mindset right before the baby arrives. There are many great books out there that walk you through everything from different stages of baby growth, physical changes in the mom-to-be, sex, birthing options, family planning, planning for college, and more. Most of these books do not offer a comprehensive walk-through on handling mental, emotional, and other psychological needs. Often, this creates a lot of negative consequences further down the line because a man who doesn't take the time to get their mind right is always going to be at a disadvantage.

Sometimes we see a young family falling apart a few months or years after the baby is born, and we assume the marriage cracked due to pressure and external factors. Did you know that in many instances, the real cause behind the fallout is internal? It's the result of unresolved mental or emotional issues that the individuals did not address.

For that simple reason, our starting point is to get you to really understand who you are... and to learn more about your wife.

It all starts with you and your childhood.

KNOWING THYSELF

Your upbringing, family, and childhood experiences shape your worldview and character. They have a profound impact on the man you become, particularly as you pick up the mantle of fatherhood. Building a family comes with unique challenges. As you face these problems, past experiences, trauma, and limiting beliefs will influence how you handle your role as a parent and husband. Many of us like to think that we are starting dadhood with a clean slate. I used to think the same until I caught myself yelling at my kid and got a flashback of my dad doing the same thing when I was a child.

The sad truth is unless you've done some "inner work" to prepare yourself emotionally, you're likely to copy-pasting much of what you experienced growing up (albeit unconscious to you). It's therefore imperative to delve deeper into yourself to uncover and resolve any lingering issues that could affect how you show up for your new family. Keep in mind that change won't occur in an instant. I'm still a work in progress, and on those rare occasions when I yell at my family, I'll immediately pause, rest, and apologize. The outbursts are less frequent, and although I'm by no means perfect, my family appreciates the work I've put into my inner work.

Every man wants to be the best for their new family but often gets hindered by invisible and past limiting beliefs. The same also applies to your wife because depending on her formative years, she might be suppressing emotional baggage that will erupt unexpectedly on you and your future child. Instead of waiting for trouble to erupt, I find it best to get proactive. Use these coming weeks and months to open dialogue between you and support each other with the pregnancy changes and the psychological transformation that needs to occur.

To help you discover, uncover, and resolve any lingering issues that might jeopardize this season of transition and your future family, there's a well-established psychological technique that you need to adopt. It's called mindfulness, and you'll do well to incorporate it into your relationship.

Before meeting your new child, you need to work on your inner child

If this is the first time you've heard the concept of the inner child, it might feel a bit spooky. This isn't some freak show, and I'm not suggesting anything that makes you look crazy in front of your wife. The topic of the inner child is pretty mainstream in the world of personal development and counseling. According to Wikipedia, the inner child is an individual's childlike aspect, and it includes what a person learned as a child before puberty. The inner child is often conceived as a semi-independent subpersonality subordinate to the waking conscious mind.

Physiotherapist Joan E. Childs has dedicated her life to studying the inner child, and she reports that *every adult has an inner child. That small part of you that just never grew up.* Regardless of how trivial, many of the wounds we experienced as children often lie dormant within just waiting for an activation trigger. You may feel like you've gotten over the hurt, but that pain will live with you for the rest of your life, and you might get unexpected reminders in your adulthood. That means that as a new parent, the stress and added responsibilities or uncertainties could trigger emotions and reactions you didn't even know existed. Why should this matter now?

Well, think about it. Having a childlike aspect within your unconscious mind that can take over when faced with a challenge means that you're likely to react not as a dad or husband but as that seven-year-old that's still scared about the unknown. Can you imagine how many unhelpful beliefs, coping mechanisms, and immature emotions that little you have?

That's why I encourage every new dad to work on healing this inner child first. Once you've uncovered and released any childhood wounds, you can reset your personality and step into the dad role as a proper adult. Those who don't invest some time to do this often find themselves further down the line reacting to challenges like a kid wearing big boy pants.

THE QUEST OF HEALING YOUR INNER CHILD

You are likely to exhibit your own family practices, beliefs, and values, as well as any unresolved issues within the context of this new family. Perhaps you've already started noticing it and if not, just ask your wife to help you identify these. It would also be best to engage in open communication to help her identify whether her inner child is showing up in your relationship. Is there anything from your families that you both don't want to be passed on to your child? What issues have you both become aware of that could be stemming from childhood experiences? Allow yourselves to be open and vulnerable with each other. Encourage your partner to reflect on her own.

HEALING EXERCISE FOR YOU AND YOUR WIFE

Aside from encouraging your wife to reflect on her family, upbringing, and childhood experiences, there are a few critical conversations you need to have in these early stages of the pregnancy. That will ensure you and your partner see eye to eye regarding the fundamental aspects of raising a child. If there is a difference, that becomes the opportunity to work together and create a game plan that aligns with your family values.

Here are some questions worth discussing.

- What are your personal views on parenting and parenthood?
- What do you think would be your parenting style?
- How do you want to raise our baby?
- What are your thoughts on religion, circumcision, vaccination, the naming of the child, and so on? These topics, while societal, can create emotional conflict if not addressed early on.

These are just a handful of questions that will point you in the right direction. Many of the answers will be influenced by childhood experiences, so if you wish to break your old patterns, it's best to have this heart-to-heart and intentionally support each other to practice conscious parenting.

BECOMING A CONSCIOUS PARENT AND THE DAD YOU DREAM OF BEING

The decision to expand your family is very emotional, and it's a good idea to develop the habit of openly discussing feelings and emotions with your partner. I can just hear your inner child yelling at how absurd that sounds because men aren't supposed to be "emotional." It's a sign of weakness, and your dad taught you that a man must never appear weak in his wife's eyes. Well, this is where you start to make new decisions about the kind of husband you're going to be. Instead of being an extension of all the fathers before you in your family line, choose to set yourself on a different path.

The transformation to a conscious dad won't happen overnight, and it will be uncomfortable at first, but with the techniques you'll pick up as you continue reading this handbook, you will achieve the objective.

MINDFULNESS AS A TOOL FOR CONSCIOUS PARENTING

You've heard me talk about conscious parenting and the necessary mindfulness practices that will become in your life. But what exactly is mindfulness? Subject matter experts define mindfulness as the basic human ability to be fully present and aware of where we are and what we are doing, not overly reactive or over-whelmed by what's happening around us. In other words, when you become mindfully present, you can fully attend to what's happening around you, what you're doing at that movement, and the space you're moving through. That might seem simple, but trust me, it is easier said than done. When you start paying close attention to your thoughts and actions, you'll soon realize how hard it is to be fully present in the moment. Our brains have this natural tendency to veer off into the future or rewind into the past. That's usually the start of all problems and the root cause of worry and anxiety. The good news is that mindfulness is a quality every human being possesses. It's not something you have to buy or pay someone for. There's no special talent for it. You just need to learn how to access it from within. The more you know and develop yourself, the easier it becomes to activate your mindfulness. Let's talk about the different ways you can begin cultivating mindfulness.

• Mindful listening

Active listening is a powerful practice that you can start cultivating as soon as today. When you engage in the various exercises shared in this guide, do your best to listen with your ears and heart. As you and your wife share vulnerable moments, be fully present and listen without judgment. Once your baby comes, listening will become even more imperative to the health of your relationship. When that baby throws a temper tantrum or your sleep-deprived wife starts complaining about how unhelpful you are in the house, don't get defensive. Instead, actively listen to what's really being communicated. Perhaps your wife starts complaining about her clothes not fitting anymore and how much she hates this thing or that person. These are opportunities for you to simply listen empathetically and provide emotional support, not "fix things." So here's a pro tip: Never ever say she looks fat. Don't even mention her growing size. Speak to how much she's glowing (even if you can't see it). And always approach her with empathy.

If she walks into the room crying, yelling, or being emotional, switch on that empathy, put down your phone/remote control/video game console or whatever you had going on and turn your gaze toward her. Give your full attention. Often that's enough to bring her back into a calm state, especially when experiencing emotional distress.

• **Mindful meditation**

Some men are huge advocates for meditation. Others can't stand it. If you've tried traditional meditation techniques that didn't work for you because you hate sitting down in a lotus position doing nothing, don't worry, I won't make you do that. There are many forms that mindfulness meditation can take. It could be in that traditional context of sitting down in silence for a specific duration. But it can also be talking about a mindfulness walk in the park or forest if you happen to live near one. You could also do your mindful meditation in the shower or with your weekly bubble bath if that's your thing. Meditation can be done anywhere at any time (yes, even in your car while sitting in traffic). In fact, the more you can find ideal scenarios to put in a few minutes of meditation, the better it will be. I know a guy who drives home, parks the car, and does a five-minute mindful meditation before entering his house. He reports that little shift has made a massive difference in the marriage because he always enters the house in the best and most relaxed mood possible, thanks to this simple technique. How long does a meditation need to last? As little as 1 minute and as long as many hours. The ideal recommended time for busy guys is between ten and twenty minutes. More important is that the length of meditation is frequency. If you can consistently pause for a set time each day at around the same time to be present and aware of yourself at that moment, you'll reap benefits you didn't even think possible. Your body chemistry will change, your immune system will improve, your sleep quality and temperament will change for the better, and your new family will notice that you are a more present, compassionate, and calm dad.

• **Mindful breathing**

The idea of mindful breathing is as simple as closing your eyes and taking deep breaths focused on nothing but the process of inhaling and exhaling. You can put your awareness on your belly and watch the movement as it expands and contracts. You can also choose to pay attention to your nose and how the air comes in and out. The main thing is to pay full attention to your breathing. Again, you can do this anywhere (the subway, office cubicle, car park, bathroom break, in bed, etc.) Pause for at least one minute or as much as five, shift your focus to your breathing, and pick a single aspect to focus on. Stay in this state of awareness until you feel your mind and body settling into a deep sense of calm and ease. From there, open your eyes and get on with the pressing matter at hand.

Live in the moment:

What all these techniques attempt to do is to assist you in being more present at the moment. That is one of the great secrets of being a great dad and husband. The present moment is the only true point of power you have, and if you can spend more time there than in the past or future, you'll have the ability to overcome negative distractions, intrusive thoughts, harmful habits, and more. It will be the secret weapon you can use to ensure your negative childhood experiences don't leak out and poison your new family.

THE KEY TAKEAWAY FOR THIS CHAPTER

- To become a great dad, the kind you wish you had growing up, you must maintain mental and emotional health. You also need to ensure your wife is self-aware and taking charge of her mental well-being.
- Investing time and effort to understand who you are, what past wounds require healing, and tending to your inner child is healthy and necessary.
- Having a heart-to-heart conversation with your wife to discuss critical issues such as her beliefs, fears, desires, and how she would wish to raise the baby will bring you closer together and ensure you're a strong team in the future.
- You must begin cultivating mindfulness in your life and identify the techniques that work best for you. By practicing mindfulness daily, you'll have the ability to catch stray thoughts and tame negative behavior before they affect your

present reality. It will also make you a better, more compassionate, and loving husband and dad.

Action plan:

Spend a few minutes noticing your frame of mind, the beliefs that came up as you read this chapter, and how you feel about your childhood. Are there things lingering in the background that need to be addressed and healed? It's time to take care of that.

Bonus New dad tip: If you're having trouble working through your emotions and inner child healing on your own, that's okay. Consider working with someone you trust or get help from a counselor or a couple's therapist if both you and your wife want to work through this together.

2

SO YOU'RE GOING TO BE A DAD— CONTEMPLATING A MILESTONE EXPERIENCE

E ven if it's the third or fourth time, becoming a dad is always scary, but for first-time dads, that fear is taunting. Don't fret over the constant smell of poop that will become the natural "scent" of your apartment. Sleep deprivation isn't also the biggest issue you'll have to deal with. Most dads have much bigger anxieties. In a Huffington Post published a while back, thirty men shared what stressed them the most about entering fatherhood. The results varied from worrying about changing diapers to worrying whether they would accidentally lose their baby in daycare and bring home a stranger. But a common theme that repeated itself in different forms was the fear of falling short either emotionally or financially.

Here are some of the responses:

> "That my children would see me as I saw myself:
> inadequate and flawed."
> "That I wouldn't know how to relate to my
> daughter."
> "Being responsible for someone else's life."
> "Financial stress."
> "Finding out it was a girl and realizing I'd have to
> pay for her wedding! Then baby number two--
> yes, also a girl. Two weddings!"

One thing is clear - if you're scared out of your mind about this new milestone, you're not alone. Remember how scared and panicked I was when my wife broke the news that baby number two was on the way? It turns out that part of my problem was that I just didn't feel prepared to take on being a daddy for another child. It isn't that I didn't want our family to grow, but I didn't have confidence in my ability to give them (all of them) the best life possible. Many first-time dads will have similar thoughts.

The good news is, I've come to understand the root cause of that reaction is confusion and lack of preparedness. So the best way to kill doubt is to prepare and build up confidence and competence. This section of the guide will walk you through an honest assessment of your values, goals, and passions. By the time you're done, you'll feel renewed in your commitment to helping your wife go through a safe and memorable pregnancy as you build your shared dream of a family.

DEALING WITH CHANGE

Change is the only constant in life, yet we struggle to embrace it. Most people experience a lot of suffering because of their resistance to change. One of the mental shifts you'll need to make right now is to hold the perspective that change is good. If nature didn't change, we'd be stuck with one season only. If babies didn't constantly change, we'd be stuck with the burden of diaper changes and an infant that only knows how to cry, poop, eat and sleep. No one wants that.

For progress and growth to take place, change must occur. Suppose you don't want to relive your childhood as a man starting a new family. In that case, you're going to need to embrace the current changes and shift from dealing with life as an immature chap to handling things like an emotionally stable, ever-evolving man. The next nine months and the first few years of your baby's life will be full of change. Everything will be unknown for you and your wife, but if you can both get on the same page, learn to embrace change, and get comfortable with being uncomfortable, you'll ride the tidal waves joyfully.

An adventure that lacks change isn't really an adventure. As the hero of your world and your family, you need to start seeing every challenge as an opportunity that adds to your hero's journey. The first couple of weeks as a pregnant couple should be devoted to intentionally creating your game plan as a new family. If you want to deal with change successfully, you'll need to set the right expectations, accept what is and develop the right mindset and attitude. Acknowledge that things are changing and it's okay. Tell yourself that as many times as needed. Realize that even good change can create stress. Some of us assume that only negative change or bad news cause stress. The truth is, even something as wonderful as having a new baby, getting a promotion you've worked so hard for, or winning the lottery brings with it new levels of stress. Take as much time as you need to adapt to the new reality but don't neglect priorities like healthy eating, rest, and intimacy. Try to keep a regular schedule as much as possible, even with the upcoming shifts in the family dynamics. It won't always be easy or even possible, but again, it's not about being perfect. It's about doing your best to maintain the structure that best serves your relationship.

A SIMPLE STRATEGY TO HELP YOU ADJUST TO THIS NEW REALITY

#1: You must make a plan.

If you think this is one of those times where you can just "wing it," you'd be sorely mistaken. Lack of preparation will be the most significant contributor to increased stress levels and overwhelm. Since we know things will dramatically change in about nine months, let's do some prep work. Start mapping out how you'll handle the prenatal visits, the logistics of the birth, baby shopping, baby's room, what you and your partner will be eating, and anything else that matters to you. Your partner will be going through significant changes with her body, which means certain things she could have done or enjoyed in the past will be out of the question now.

Be mindful of these changes. Are there certain foods your wife can't stand anymore? Take them out of the menu. Adjust your schedule to support her as best as you can without compromising your well-being and work. These changes will likely carry over into the initial phases post-childbirth, so remain flexible with your plans. Get ready to be more proactive in the daily affairs of running the home, at least until your wife is back to her old, energetic self once the baby is gone.

The change will feel less stressful when you have a clearly outlined plan and several contingency plans in place. It doesn't mean you'll foresee all that could happen over the next year, but just as a good business owner must create a plan for navigating their new start-up, you'd be wise to have a plan that enables you to feel more capable of handling this new norm.

#2: Reframe your thinking. Every situation is only as good or as bad as your thinking makes it.

You should write that statement on your bathroom mirror. It's time to become the master of your mental space. When those feelings of overwhelm, anxiety, stress, and negativity creep in, you need to pause and give your brain a time-out. The very fact that you're aware of the negative emotion or thought means you can reframe the current situation or problem so that it becomes an opportunity instead of a crisis. So, for example, instead of entertaining the fear of being a bad father or failing to provide and protect your young family, tweak these thoughts into "I am a hard-working man with a great job, and I know I'll do my best to be the dad I always wanted." Instead of worrying about your intimacy dying out, think, "I deserve a happy marriage, and I know my wife and I will find a way to make things great." These simple shifts in your thinking and how you approach any unpleasant topic make a difference. That's one of the techniques I used to shift from panic and anxiety into joy as we prepared to add baby number two to our family. Finances were one of my biggest concerns at the time. Instead of allowing myself to wallow in self-pity and the fear of not making ends meet for my family, I decided to become proactive. Knowing my hard work ethos and my growing skills, I was determined to get a better job, find new ways to increase income, and more. We'll talk about all these ideas in the next chapter.

#3: Put everything down in writing.

Let's use the idea of a start-up company once more. If you're an entrepreneur who wants to succeed long-term, experts will advise you to write a business plan and your product development and marketing strategy. Documenting your game plan is critical in any successful endeavor, and that's what I'm encouraged to do with your new family. Have a sit down with your wife after the initial heart-to-heart that we discussed earlier and document things that matter. That may include healthy habits that you wish to incorporate, financial plans, budgets, and more. Some couples use this time to square out basic duties such as who will be responsible for the pets (if you have any), meal preps, housekeeping, etc. If you or your wife are currently studying, make sure to clear up any upcoming exams and perhaps even allow yourself some time off because those first couple of weeks after delivery might be too chaotic to keep up with studies. Many parents report how impossible it is to keep up with school and exams when there's barely enough time to sleep or think once the baby arrives. So consider this.

Every household will have different needs, so be sure to customize your plan accordingly. You should also get into the habit of reflecting on your written goals daily and perhaps even monitoring your most dominant emotions week by week. Mindfulness experts recommend keeping a private journal next to your bed so you can have a place to express yourself instead of suppressing emotions. I prefer to have a bedside A4 writing pad where I do a couple of things daily. First, I write out the goals we are moving toward as a family every morning. Then I invest a few minutes naming the things I am grateful for. Lastly, before sleeping each night, I write out the emotions that filled my day - both positive and negative. Over time, I start to get a sense of my mental and emotional state so that I don't B.S myself into thinking things are good when if they're not. Gathering this data has made a huge difference in my life, and the best part, these activities take no more than 5 minutes. Surely, even you can get five minutes in the morning and another five in the evening!

#4: Maintain open communication and give yourself lots of room for flexibility.

It doesn't matter how bulletproof your plan is, it won't go precisely as documented, and that's okay. You might have a month-by-month plan actioned out, and then the baby comes four weeks early. Now, what?!? Or you might be planning a normal "at-home birth," and then two weeks to the due date, the doctor insights that for medical reasons and the baby's safety, cesarean birth is the best alternative. What the heck, man?!?

And just like that, your finances get a terrible hit. All this to say, your plan needs a lot of legroom. It's good to plan, but it's even better to plan to know that you can handle the unexpected as well without losing your grip on things. Your ability to remain flexible and grounded throughout this period is determined by how well your communication is with your wife. If you've planned together, shared fears, desires, goals, vision, and you continue to keep each other in the loop daily, then together, there's nothing you won't overcome. In fact, any emergency will only make your relationship and teamwork stronger.

WE'RE PREGNANT!

From now on, I want you always to say "we're preg-nant" instead of "she's pregnant." Why? Because whether or not the spotlight is on you (and it never is), you still play an integral role in this family adventure. No two couples will ever have the same experiences; heck, no two pregnancies will ever be the same. All my babies were different both during the pregnancy and their first years of growth. The actual journey of going from fetus to newborn baby is no walk in the park and will have its fair share of excitement and difficulties. These next few months will demand so much from you mentally, emotionally, and physically. That applies to both you and your partner. The more knowledgeable you are about the different phases of pregnancy and what to expect, the easier it will be to remain calm, supportive of each other, and make informed decisions.

Where does the dad-to-be fit in?

I know it can be hard to hold a supportive role and lovingly take the backseat as your wife receives all the attention during pregnancy. Yet that's precisely what I'm asking you to do. While she's pregnant, the spot-light will always be on her. As soon as your newborn arrives, all the attention will shift to accommodate both of them. But just because our society hasn't evolved (yet) to naturally create a spot for the supportive dad doesn't mean you don't deserve the credit.

The world may not easily see all the work you do but trust me, your new family will know and appreciate all that you do in the background. Research shows that women who receive unconditional support from their partners during pregnancy tend to have lower stress levels. So I need you to work on reframing what certain things mean to you. If you start feeling neglected, left out, or rejected, pause for a moment and deal with that negativity. Chances are, your wife is just consumed by all the hormonal, physical, and psychological changes that need to take place.

It's also important to set the right expectations. For example, if your prenatal or antenatal care is still traditional and not very accomodating to you as a modern dad, don't take it personally. It's easy to feel invisible if a health professional talks as if your wife is the only one going through this experience. A friend recently shared that during his first antenatal visits, he felt like there was a general sense of "dude, you've done your part, now leave the rest to us." Some hospitals tend to come across that way, and if it bothers you so much, talk to your wife and see if you can find a better, more involved solution.

Again, let me emphasize, this isn't one of those movie scenes where a stranger walks into a pub, and everyone's local, and they look at him as an outsider. It's as much your adventure as it is your wife's. Be vocal about your desire to be as involved as possible. Let her know how little or how much you want to participate at every phase of the pregnancy, delivery, and early years of childhood development. That way, you can choose health professionals who can facilitate that experience.

Some of the things you can do to make this period as memorable and pleasant as possible include open communication with your wife so she can feel comfortable enough to share with you her experience. You should also let her know the responsibilities you want to take on to ease the stress she has to deal with. I recommend you attend as many doctor visits as you can so you can see your baby's growth and development. One thing that increases my sense of connection to my unborn child is hearing the heartbeat for the first time. There's nothing quite like that moment. You can also take the initiative in changing some of the activities and eating habits you and your wife do so you can move toward a more healthy pregnancy together. For example, make time to go for walks together and encourage her to eat more nutritious food. These small things are done as a couple increase your bond and make it easier for the soon-to-be mom to adjust her lifestyle in preparation for motherhood. We'll talk more about the different ways you can show support at each stage of the pregnancy in upcoming sections of the guide.

OVERCOMING THE FEAR OF BEING A NEW DAD

There's nothing wrong with being a worried expectant father. Fear is something you'll need to contend with at some point, and it's part of every great hero's journey. The good news is, the more you face your fears, the easier it will be to transition into a beneficial role as a dad and husband. Many of the fears we all have are around money, upheaval in life, relationships, and whether or not we can live up to the expectations of others. Let's boldly address some of these fears and what to do about them.

• **Do I have what it takes to be a great dad?**

Men struggle with this thought because there is no binary answer. Raising a child is a lifelong experience, and there's no single test one can take to be declared a great dad. A fear many expectant fathers have is whether or not they have what it takes to step into real adulthood.

Can you make the personal sacrifices that your wife and baby will require? Are you ready to stop living a self-focused life?

A great dad makes all his decisions thinking about how it impacts his family's future. That's not something men naturally do, even if they are in a serious relationship, and it takes a conscious decision and lots of practice.

So if in your quiet time, you keep coming back to this question, rest easy. You're not the first man to question your ability to be the kind of father your kid will be proud of.

What to do:

Take it one day, one step at a time. During the pregnancy, focus on being the best and most supportive husband or partner you can be. It's all about the choices you make daily. Once the baby is born, apply the same approach. If you have the choice between Saturday football and dinner with your new family, choose wisely. As the baby grows, decide to be involved each day. If you have a boy and you find him outside throwing a ball on his own, instead of throwing yourself in front of the TV, choose to join him outside and play catch no matter how lousy he is. If your young daughter is obsessed with dolls and brushing their hair, sit on the living room carpet and do that. We tend to assume that being a great dad is a one-size-fits-all or that there's one thing you could do that will make you a great dad. The truth is, the little things you do consistently are what determines what kind of a dad you become. And the only thing you need to have right now is the determination to be the best version of yourself.

- **How will I know what to do if something goes wrong?**

There are many things you won't have control over in the coming months, and most of the things you'll see and experience will be scary. Some dads actually pass out because of how overwhelming the childbirth experience is. Whether it's during pregnancy, childbirth, or the first few months of the baby's arrival, you will face a lot of uncomfortable experiences. Things may not go exactly as planned, no matter how great the game plan is.

What to do:

Stay calm and focus on the things you can control. Your mental and emotional state is always in your control. If you can keep your mind grounded in the bigger picture and you've done enough prep work, you'll ride any unexpected wave. If the childbirth process overwhelms you, consider enrolling with your wife in a childbirth class and get focused on how you can help as her coach.

Going through the process before it actually happens will make the entire process more tolerable, and you'll have a better idea of what you can do in different scenarios.

- **Can I afford to have a new baby?**

I asked myself this question with the coming of every new baby. Trust, me, I thought there was no way I could afford a second baby. These little ones come with hefty costs, from clothing to diapers and baby food. My wife is often in the habit of shopping for the cutest things, but the baby only wears them for a few weeks before outgrowing them. It makes no sense! Instead of fighting this fact, accept that you will need to make some financial sacrifices.

What to do:

1. Become a little more creative with your baby shopping and budget as much as you can.
2. Be proactive in helping your wife make the right shopping decisions.
3. Don't let her excitement about those tiny onesies and booties hurt your finances.

Thanks to eCommerce stores, you can also get incredible deals for baby stuff if you do some comprehensive online research.

The bottom line is this: Your work-life balance will be significantly impacted, and the next few years will require some adjustments in your intimacy and the kind of relationship you've grown accustomed to. As time goes on, things will feel more stable if you've done the groundwork within yourself and with the support structures you create around the family dynamic. We'll dive into more details as the book unfolds, but I hope by now you're feeling less stressed about the changes that are about to happen. Parenting is a tremendous job, but it's one of the most rewarding things you will ever do. Sure, you can't be out partying and drinking with the boys every weekend. And yes, you do need to prep yourself for very little intimacy (at least for a time), but if you allow nature to take its natural course and just flow with this new role of being a dad, you'll find life becomes more rewarding and fulfilling than ever before.

THE KEY TAKEAWAY FOR THIS CHAPTER:

- You'll need to prepare yourself emotionally for this significant role. And it's okay if you experience doubt, overwhelm, and even fear.
- Change is always hard (even good change), but this particular change will turn you into the best version of yourself if you let it. Your

attitude, mindset, and expectations will determine your reality.

- Although the spotlight is always going to be on your pregnant wife and then shift to the new baby, later on, the role you play is integral to their well-being and happiness. Never forget that.
- Choose to be a hands-on dad and become as involved as possible starting today. Let your wife know that you are there for her, and she can count on you no matter what. Even when you don't understand her needs, just be there. Sometimes, it's as simple as listening with your head and heart.
- Fear will come knocking if it hasn't yet. That's okay. Every dad worries about their inadequacies, whether the time is right, and whether they can make their kid proud. This is nothing new. The antidote to this fear is to get your game plan going and to commit to consistently being the best man, husband, and father you can be. One day, one step at a time is all you need to focus on.

Action plan:

Spend some time in reflection now before moving to the next chapter and answer the following questions:

- What's one small thing you can do today to affirm your new status as the best new dad in the world?
- What fear came up for you as you went through this chapter? Did any of the ones mentioned ring a bell? How can you start working through some of the fears that you're now aware of? Could you journal them out and then describe what you'd want to experience instead? Could you share these with your wife or even a professional so you can overcome them?
- How worried are you about finances? Do you feel like you have a working plan to help you navigate the next few months? What about the next few years?

3

EMOTIONAL HEALTH FOR PARENTS DURING PREGNANCY AND AFTER BIRTH

Y ou and your wife should prioritize mental health during the perinatal period (the period covering pregnancy and the first year following the baby's birth). Why? Because according to various reports, plenty of dads are struggling with mental well-being. 24%-50% of new dads with partners suffering from depression were also affected by depression themselves (Goodman, 2004). Up to 38% of new dads are worried about their mental health (NCT), and worse still, an average of 10.4% of fathers are depressed both pre-and-post natally, with the peak time for father's depression being between three and six months post-birth (Paulson & Brazemore, 2010).

Feelings, relationships, and how they impact pregnancy should be addressed, but few of us take the time to do it. Most people only focus on the obvious things like finances, the woman's physical changes, her cravings, and so on. And while all these things are important (and we'll talk about them in upcoming chapters as well), it's equally vital to discuss your emotional well-being. You and your wife need to look after yourselves and recognize where you might need a little extra support to be mentally and emotionally prepared for the upcoming changes.

HOW ARE YOU FEELING?

Little is known about the needs and mental health experiences that new fathers face, and the methods used for detecting depression in fathers before and after the birth of their child are limited. You'll notice that everyone will be concerned about your wife's emotional state, but hardly anyone will remember to ask you. Moving into the father role can bring a lot of anxiety. If you feel isolated, underappreciated and overwhelmed, or fearful of the changes and responsibilities that await you, the risk of mental illness significantly increases. Most of the time, socioeconomic factors like income, living conditions, and unemployment can accelerate mental health issues. Fear of inadequacy can also significantly affect how you feel about the pregnancy and your abilities as a providing father figure.

Some first-time dads have described themselves as feeling like a "bystander" to the mother-infant bond and more removed than they had imagined. To ensure you don't fall into any unhealthy emotional states, we need to train your brain to become resilient.

One of the best things you can do for your mental well-being and sense of competency as a new dad is to educate yourself more about pregnancy, childcare, and your role as a dad. Reading this book is one of the first steps toward that growth mindset. It's also essential to understand and prepare for the potential relationship changes or pressures you might experience with your wife.

Suppose you notice yourself struggling to be optimistic about your life and the pregnancy, and you notice changes in appetite, lack of motivation, a significant drop in concentration, and feelings of guilt and worthlessness. In that case, it's time to take action. Let your wife know that you're experiencing some mental imbalances, and then immediately talk to a qualified professional or, at the very least, get a mindset coach to help you push past this phase.

Once the baby arrives, stay vigilant and keep feeding your mind the right stuff but even then, if you feel the burden is too heavy, talk to your wife and be prepared to get external help.

I want to add that it can be advantageous to surround yourself with a specific support group of dads. You can find such a group in your local area or join our Facebook virtual group because sometimes, having a safe space where you can talk to others who recently went through what you're going through can give you that mental boost needed to stay on the right mental track. This period of your life will be a massive test of your relationship with yourself and your wife. You will need mental resilience and strategies that can help you build emotional strength so your family's well-being and your own don't get compromised. Be open to the fact that having a new baby can be stressful, and it is, therefore, crucial you give yourself the time, self-care, and support needed to keep you in good health. Don't be afraid to ask for and receive help from your wife, loved ones, and your dad's support group.

YOUR EMOTIONS AND RELATIONSHIP WITH YOUR PARTNER

This is your first baby, so it's okay when you find yourself struggling with new emotions. Sometimes you might lash out a little at a poor waiter or even your wife and maybe get into an argument over very trivial things. Couples commonly have these experiences in the early stages of raising a family. You need to know that it's your job to take care of your emotions and bring back that sense of calm to your mind. Failure to do this means those arguments will increase in frequency and ultimately drive a wedge between you when you should be working on being closer and more loving.

A few things you can do to nurture a healthy mental and emotional state include:

- Invest in mindset training that helps you develop your mental resilience so you can feel confident about facing any challenge as it comes.
- Talking to your wife about how you're feeling. Allow yourself to be vulnerable about the things that excite you and those that scare you.
- Be open and honest about your sexual needs. Listen to her as well as she shares how she feels about your intimacy so you can find practical ways of ensuring you're both happy during this period.
- Play a more active role during the pregnancy, birth, and after the child is born. You are not insignificant as a dad. You are just as much a parent to this baby as your wife. Read that last part several times until it sinks in. Once you

feel and believe that, everyone around you will start seeing you that way.

If you don't feel any emotional shifts yet, that's okay too. For some men, the reality of parenthood doesn't kick in until the baby is born. Then the shock hits, leaving the guy feeling paralyzed.

YOUR WIFE'S EMOTIONS DURING PREGNANCY

Pregnancy is fascinating and challenging all at once. It's normal for expectant moms and dads to experience some ups and downs while moving through the nine months and early years of raising a child. Your wife will certainly have her fair share of emotional unrest, especially as her hormones shift into overdrive in the coming months. But chronic anxiety and worry aren't normal, and that could end up affecting both your lives even after birth. So exercise plenty of mindfulness, and should you notice your wife experiencing severe mood swings, panic attacks, obsessive-compulsive behavior, too much fear, constant sadness, and crying for no apparent reason, please talk to your doctor or midwife. Once in a while, you might see those emotions flaring up, but they should never last more than two weeks at a time.

YOUR WIFE'S INTERNAL STATE AND THE DEVELOPMENT OF YOUR UNBORN CHILD

Did you know that your wife's emotional state affects the growing fetus? Throughout history, wise women elders in different cultures have always advised new moms to watch their internal states diligently during pregnancy. But it was never considered scientific until recently. Animal studies have shown that maternal stress can affect offspring, but that's just with animals, right? Well, a little over a decade ago, research on human mothers and babies started showing similar results. Stress, anxiety, and depression can and do alter a child's development with long-lasting consequences.

That's not to say that your wife should never experience any kind of stress. We don't want her to turn into a passive couch potato. What we're aiming for is just the right amount of stress that can help her function optimally. Researcher at John Hopkins University Janet DiPietro says the human brain requires sufficient but not overwhelming stress to promote optimal neural development both before and after birth. Pietro and colleagues studied pregnant women who were mentally healthy, well-educated, and had low-risk pregnancies. Midway through the pregnancy, Pietro measured the level of the mother's psychological distress. After the babies were born, she tested their development at six weeks and again at two years. The results were interesting. Pietro found that babies whose mothers had mild to moderate distress were more advanced in physical and mental development.

But what does that mean? Should your wife welcome stress to boost fetal development?

Absolutely not. According to DiPietro, the everyday stress of modern living is more than enough. The last thing a new mom needs is to head into caring for a newborn with mounting pressure, abuse, and constant anxiety. I will go out on a limb and say your current lifestyle provides ample stress for your wife and growing baby to develop enough resilience to ensure the baby develops fast after birth.

That leads me to an all-important study conducted by a well-known obstetrician, Christiane Northrup, in 2005. Northrup found that if a pregnant woman experiences high levels of fear or anxiety, she creates a metabolic cascade. Hormones known as cytokines are produced, and the mother's immune system is affected, directly affecting the unborn child. If, however, the mother is feeling healthy and happy, she produces oxytocin. The presence of this hormone creates feelings of bonding and strengthens immunity in the baby. Neurotransmitters moving inside the mother's body make a chemical and physical imprint on the baby's brain and body with messages of safety and peace. So if you think your unborn child isn't already developing a framework to deal with the outside world, think again. In fact, in the upcoming chapter where I break down the week-by-week progress, you'll be shocked to learn how early on your baby learns to feel, taste, learn and have some level of consciousness. And what they experience while in the womb shapes who they become as they grow into teenhood and adulthood.

Why you should care:

Too much stress on your wife is the real danger when it comes to fetal development. When women experience severe stress during pregnancy, their babies are at risk of developing severe health problems. In studies on pregnant women, intense stress such as losing a loved one, war, earthquakes, floods, fire, terrorist attacks, and interpersonal violence have been linked to terrible outcomes. These include premature birth, low birth weight, and even miscarriage. Pregnant women who experience chronic stress like homelessness and discrimination were likely to give birth to babies with respiratory and digestive problems, irritability, or sleep problems. They are also more apt to experience developmental problems with cognitive, behavioral, social-emotional, and health issues that suggest neurodevelopmental changes that ripple into adolescence and adulthood.

A woman who experiences depression during pregnancy is also a concern because she's four times more likely to have a low birth weight and more prone to postpartum depression. Postpartum depression is a massive challenge for any family, and we'll talk more about that and how to support your wife and newborn in a follow-up book series that deals with the first few years of parenthood. For now, however, here's what you need to remember.

How you treat your wife over the coming weeks and months will directly influence her emotions and, by default, impact the unborn child. Be mindful of the environment, energy, and dominant state that your wife experiences. Don't be the source of her overwhelm, anguish or sadness, as that will directly impact the baby. The opposite is also true. If you can become a source of joy, positivity, encouragement, and love for your wife, that too will impact her emotional state and, in turn, affect how the fetus develops. You might not have realized how important your role is. Still, I hope by now you're starting to see that although this baby isn't developing inside your body, you still have the power to influence its well-being and development positively. How cool is that?

THE TAKEAWAY FROM THIS CHAPTER:

- Mental well-being should be a priority for both you and your wife.
- • Although most people only focus on the mom's mental state, your mental well-being matters greatly. It's important to regularly check in with yourself to see how healthy you feel emotionally.
- If you notice either you or your wife are exhibiting symptoms of distress or mental illness that persist for over two weeks, seek help. Openly share what's happening and reach out to a qualified professional, a mindset coach, or your support group, depending on how much help you feel is needed.
- Be vulnerable and share with each other both positives and negatives about this experience. Openly talk about your intimacy and how this will change over the coming months. Figure out your needs and make your wife aware so you can map out a plan of action that keeps your relationship intact. Don't make assumptions about your sex life.
- What your wife feels directly impacts your baby's development in utero. Therefore, choose to become a source of joy, good energy, and

support for your wife, as that will directly influence how your baby grows long after birth.

Action plan:

Start a private journal and observe your emotions over the next seven days. Notice how often you feel positive versus negative emotions. Are you leaning more on the negative side? Is it leaking out to your relationships and conversations? How often are you having disagreements with the people in your life? How are you really feeling about this pregnancy? How are you treating your wife daily, and what emotions do you typically evoke from her? Take some time to reflect and then make some adjustments where needed.

One more thing you can do here is to become aware of the needs you have and make it a point to discuss these with your wife on your next date night. With that taken care of, the next thing to prioritize is your finances. After all, our emotions get flared up all the more when we feel financially insecure.

4

PRIORITIZING FINANCIAL HEALTH

W e all know how cute tiny clothes and heartwarming ultrasound photos can be for pregnant couples, and it's great to enjoy those moments. But if you want to remain sane and in control of your family's future, we need to address the elephant in the room - Finances.

Having a baby is pretty expensive regardless of where you live. It's not a topic many couples like to have until things become tough and money runs out, but it's one I encourage you to have as early on in the family planning or pregnancy as possible. Getting on the same page with your partner when it comes to spending and saving money that caters to your new family is vital for a healthy relationship and happy family life.

I'd like to start this chapter by prefacing the fact that I am not a financial advisor or economist, so the best I can do is encourage you to seek technical information from certified experts. Also, we need to bear in mind that costs tend to fluctuate over time depending on your place of residence, so as you read this book, customize it to suit your earnings, lifestyle, cost of living, and the current health care situation you're in.

According to a 2017 report from the U.S Department of Agriculture (USDA), a middle-class American married couple spends an average of $296,684 (approximately $17,500 per year) on raising a child from birth to age 18. And that's not inclusive of college tuition and the costs associated with higher education. That's a big number, especially if you have no financial strategy going into parenthood. Wouldn't you agree?

Although it may not seem like it, the small purchases here and there will eventually add up and become overwhelming if you don't get ahead of things. Nothing is more important for your peace of mind as a new parent than knowing how to manage your expectations and expenses. Many experts say that new parents start to feel the pinch right when the baby is six months old. And that's usually when the fighting starts and cracks in the marriage become visible.

The good news is that you can head off that looming trouble by committing to a financial plan immediately. Research shows that given the same income, couples who come up with a good plan and stick to it save twice as much money as those who just wing it!

LET'S TALK FINANCES

The fact is, there's a lot to think about. You and your partner need to consider where you live, which doctors you're going to go for, what quality of life you're going to maintain, and so much more. If you already have insurance and you live in a state that isn't too expensive, then it's estimated that you might spend as low as $4,000 (depending on what your insurance covers).

A new mother once told me that she had refused to get off her contraceptives until her husband bought them the right insurance coverage so their finances would be a bit more manageable once she got pregnant. Now that's a financially determined housewife!

If you live in America, you need to realize that certain states are more favorable for baby-making, whether you have insurance or not. But in every state, the cost significantly rises if one doesn't have insurance. Some couples end up spending close to $11,000 for a vaginal delivery without insurance. But this is only if there are no complications. If you include care provided before and after pregnancy, including checkups and tests, then you're likely looking at a total of $30,000.

According to recent reports, C-sections are becoming more frequent compared to a few decades ago. That means more bills to pay. How much more? C-section births cost from $7,500 - $14,500, which does not include all the other costs such as prenatal care, obstetrician's fee, etc. It also doesn't include what happens after you bring the baby into the world, and it assumes that the baby is 100% healthy, needing no extra medical attention.

EXPENSES TO EXPECT

Again, these numbers will vary depending on your state and whether or not you've got insurance coverage. Records show that hospitals typically charge uninsured patients more than those covered by private and public plans. Suppose you live in Alabama, then it's likely your lowest cost would be about $4,884 for a vaginal delivery with insurance and about $9013 without. On the other hand, if you live in Alaska, you can expect to foot a bill of about $10,681 with coverage and $19,775 without insurance. Crazy right? Okay, so you need to start researching and figuring out your exact costs, but a good starting point is to look at the list below of the basic services your wife will need and the estimated costs you can expect to see.

OBGYN appointments (even if you switch to a midwife later on) will be an average of seven to twelve prenatal visits in total. In addition to the visits, your wife will also need to do a series of tests.

- Doctor's visits can range anywhere from $90 - $500 per appointment.
- hCG test might be around $40.
- Ultrasound will range between $280 - $600.
- Amniocentesis is about $2500.
- Blood tests range between $39 - $63 each.
- Chorionic Villus Sampling (CVS) ranges from $1,300 - $4,800.

You should also know that after the baby is born, both your wife and child will need postpartum care, which means additional costs. Average it up to about $3,100 if you've got insurance. These costs can be overwhelming, especially if you don't get yourself sorted with some kind of medical cover and you happen to live in a state with high costs of delivery and childcare.

If you live in other parts of the world, your costs might be lower or higher than what we experience in the U.S, but I doubt it will be cheap. Unless, of course, you live in Canada, the United Kingdom, or Australia, where they have varying healthcare systems that make it free, almost free, or relatively affordable to have a child if one is a citizen of the nation. Based on my limited research, only Americans need to cough out hefty sums to bring a baby into the world. My recommendation is to get insurance immediately. We'll talk about how shortly.

With thousands of dollars going into pregnancy care and childbirth, we need to figure out how you can start tightening up that budget so you can be more financially mobile and confident enough to handle whatever comes. Here's what I know for sure. A man's worst nightmare is not knowing where the money will come from if an emergency occurs. If all you have is just enough to get by, that fear of the unknown will turn your hair gray and deprive you of sleep faster than the tantrums of a toddler. If you think not having sex or lack of sleep is your biggest concern, think again. I can't tell you how many times I've talked to guys who retold the nightmare they experienced when they procrastinated on their finances only to get to week 37 and receive that emergency call from the OBGYN saying, *"Bill, we need you to come in and sign for an emergency C-section."* To keep both baby and mom safe, Bill has to consent. Suddenly, his financial projections fail, and he's taunted by the fear of losing mom or baby and the burden of paying an enormous bill after the fact. It's hell on earth, my friend, and an experience I wouldn't wish on my worst enemy. What you need is a solid plan.

THE 10-STEP APPROACH OF COVERING YOUR NEW FAMILY'S FINANCIAL NEEDS

#1: Budgeting for the new arrival.

You should do this in the first trimester. You can work with a financial consultant if you're feeling lost so they can help you create a financial plan that suits your needs. This is also the time to clean up your financial activities, and there's no better place to start than with credit card bills. You and your wife need to come clean and figure out how much you owe and the best way to manage those interests. Perhaps you need to transfer your balance to a credit card with lower interest rates.

You should also track all your spending now that you've created a new budget. Big and small expenses need to be tracked so you can have a better picture of your monthly spending. Use a spreadsheet, a phone app, or whatever you prefer. Track things for about three months, after which you'll need to crunch the numbers. That's when you'll identify spending patterns so you can see the areas to cut back on once the baby arrives.

For example, if you eat out three nights a week, try to cut back to once a week. Once that becomes a habit, shift focus to another area where you can save money. I also encourage you to check prices for diapers, baby food, formula, clothing, bedding, and any other items that you'll repeatedly need to have a cost estimate. Don't forget to include the extra laundry detergent and any babysitting costs you'll incur when you take the Mrs. out for date night (yes, this needs to be prioritized. Otherwise, you're killing any chance of rekindling the romance in those early months).

#2: Drafting pre-baby budget.

Adjust your existing budget accordingly once you've estimated what you'll be spending on medical bills and baby essentials. Babies come with plenty of expenses, so make sure you set tight limits. Don't allow you or your wife to go gaga over baby equipment. Trust me. Your baby doesn't care about designer diaper bags or a stroller with LCD control panels that are trendy. If the car seat and stroller meet safety standards, you're good to go.

Suppose you feel you've recorded enough data on your past spending. In that case, it's time to put everything on a budget tracking app so you can figure out what the new family budget (taking into consideration the monthly spending of the new baby) will be. Your goal here isn't just to eliminate unnecessary expenses and accommodate new baby needs but also to save for emergencies, future costs, and whatever other long-term financial goals you might have. According to a 2015 USDA report, the average middle-income household can expect to spend about $1056 each month to provide an infant with the basics (food, shelter, clothing, transportation, and childcare). The last thing you should do is stress-test this new family budget to see if you can stay within the identified limitations even before the baby arrives.

#3: Maximise your emergency savings.

Do you currently have an existing "rainy day" fund? Great. It's time to double down your savings efforts. If not, what the heck are you waiting for, man?!? I can almost guarantee you'll need this at some point within the next 12 months because new families come with all kinds of unforeseen medical emergencies. Work to get in place at least three to six months' worth of living expenses covered, and that should at least give you some breathing room in case sh** hits the fan.

#4: Update your health insurance.

If you don't have health insurance, now is the time to get it. Often it's easier to get coverage through you or your wife's employer, but when that's not a possibility, you can also look into insurance offered through the Affordable Care Act. Talk to a professional insurance broker to get you the best option that works for your current situation. But make sure you have some kind of insurance, especially if you are an American starting your family in America. Health insurance is one of the best ways to bring down the cost of pregnancy, childbirth, and the early years of postnatal care.

#5: Apply for prenatal leave.

How much time do you and your partner have for prenatal care? Is it paid leave? The answer you give influences your finances significantly. A large majority of American workers, unfortunately, don't have access to paid family leave. So, suppose you're a single-income household, and your company doesn't have a favorable policy. In that case, this is something you'll need to discuss with your wife because taking time off from work once the baby arrives may not be ideal for your finances.

On the other hand, perhaps you both work, but your wife gets very little paid maternity leave. In which case, you might come to an agreement that it's okay for her to take more time for the baby while you handle finances for a while. Federal law requires you to give at least a 30-day notice when requesting time off under the Family and Medical Leave Act. This law also entitles any new parent who works for a company with at least 50 employees to take up to 12 weeks of unpaid, seniority-protected leave. Your employer must pay the usual portion of your healthcare benefits for the duration. But again, figure out what policies are adhered to at your company and then do the math to see what you can or cannot afford to do.

#6: Consider getting life insurance and disability insurance.

If one of both income earners is unable to work and generate a monthly income for any reason, that infant will experience a lot of difficulty growing up. That's why many couples look into getting "term life insurance" and the appropriate kind of disability insurance. The term life insurance is a kind of insurance that's often affordable and expires after a set term, typically anywhere between 10 - 30 years. Both of these can be great safety nets should something happen to you and/or your wife after birth. But if you had to choose one, I'd say go for disability insurance because you're far likely to need it. Talk to your insurance broker to learn more and evaluate your options.

#7: Start evaluating childcare options.

If you're already in the third trimester, that might be a great time to start discussing prenatal solutions and child care options, especially if your wife has a full-time career. Think about the costs of various facilities compared to hiring in-house nannies. Of course, this will vary depending on your finances and needs. Maybe you have a sister-in-law who loves pets and kids but can't seem to hold a job. It might be time to let her move in for a few months just to give you guys an extra hand. If you're fortunate enough to have a great mom or mother-in-law, consider leaning into those options as well. Excellent childcare doesn't have to be expensive or sourced from strangers. Be creative with your solutions and find what works best.

#8: Add your child to your health insurance within the first 30 days of the baby's birth.

While the new mom and baby get comfortable with their new environments, it's a wise decision to include the new family member into your health policy. Babies need a lot of hospital visits, so the best practice is to add them sooner rather than later. Most insurance policies have a due date, often between 30-60 days, where you are required to register your child, so please prioritize this because you don't want to get caught with a sick baby and no coverage. It's a headache no new dad should have to deal with, especially if they were smart enough to get insurance pre-baby.

NEW DAD | 75

#9: Get a social security number for your child.

Did you know having a baby can help you save money at tax time? Talk about turning that baby into a contributing member of the family from the get-go. Once the baby is born, you'll need to get a birth certificate issued. With this document, you can also request an SSN at the hospital, which is great because that's all you need to claim various income tax deductions and credits. Talk to your accountant about this if you'd like to understand the details of how to make this happen.

#10: Start saving for future expenses.

I know this might sound strange, but you do need to think about your child's future. If you recall the estimated costs I shared of raising and educating a child, it should make sense that you'll need to set aside a little money for those future expenses. Your kid will likely want gadgets (every 9-year old seems to need a smartphone and a TikTok account), music lessons, summer camp, themed parties, and more. I could go on, but I think you get it.

Once you've stabilized immediate needs, i.e., the family budget and your emergency funds, I highly recommend starting a future expense account for the new baby. Most parents like to do this after the first birthday.

GETTING ON THE SAME PAGE

Money and mindset go hand in hand in relationships, and the best couples know the importance of working on both -together. Given your different backgrounds and experiences with money, it's impossible that things will automatically click when it comes to money management. So you'll need to try different ways to manage finances before arriving at the method that aligns with both of you. Discuss the various options you'll test (combining finances, keeping things separate, having a joint account, etc.) and be prepared for plenty of trial and error at the beginning. If money is an emotional trigger which it often is, invest some time changing your beliefs around money.

Did you know about 70% of married couples argue about money? A study found that the most common points of disagreement among couples when it comes to money are: major purchases (34%), a partner's spending habit (23%), and important investment decisions (14%). (Budgetbakers - How to manage your money together as a couple).

One of the most important things you can do with your partner is get honest about money and how you spend it. If you can make that your starting point, it won't be too difficult to find the best way for both of you to handle finances. Before worrying about how open your wife is to showing you what she does with her credit card, realize that carrying a baby changes all women. She might have been an impulsive, reckless spender, buying a new pair of shoes on Amazon every week but now that a new family is on the horizon, you'll start seeing a change in her. She will admire you greatly for your newfound zeal for taking a handle on money to secure your family's future. A few of the things you should be discussing in these first few weeks of pregnancy can include:

• **Sharing expenses**

How do you want to split the responsibility of paying for expenses and saving? It's important to agree on how to split the bills and who takes responsibility to pay which bill. Some couples prefer to split things equally when it comes to expenses. Others prefer to make that decision based on income. That way, the person who earns more gets to cover the larger percentage, and the lesser income earner contributes based on their earnings. I have also seen couples who agree to share expenses as per usage. That way, the higher income earner doesn't resent their partner for spending all their money. In this set-up, both of you would pay things like rent and utility bills together, but other things like phone bills, gym fees, beauty treatments, and other personal uses would be covered by the respective partner. Of course, this makes things a bit more complex to execute, but with proper planning and the right tools, it can work. Savings can also be approached using one of these options depending on financial goals. Most couples have both shared and individual goals to which they contribute separately. Test drive the structure that most aligns with you. Don't be afraid to switch to something else if things go awry.

- **The three best options for handling family finances**

The three best options for managing money are separate accounts, joint accounts, or a combination of both. Couples like separate accounts when they aren't very comfortable sharing every aspect of their finances. It can help clarify income disparities, debts, and potential spender-versus-saver personality conflicts. A huge benefit of going this route is that each of you remains 100% responsible for your spending and saving habits. What matters is strong communication about when and how you will take care of the shared bills. The downside to this option is that you'll need to keep tabs on your wife a lot, especially if she's a spender. Things will get even more hectic when the baby arrives.

Things are a little easier with a joint account because you can easily track budgets on a spreadsheet or budgeting software. There's no monthly division of resources, and even with the baby's arrival, all expenses will continue flowing from that family account. That makes the adjustment to family life less stressful. Unfortunately, if you're like most men, you'll start losing sleep when you discover your wife spends ridiculous money on things that have no value. I have a friend who once shared that discovering how much time his wife spends mobile shopping caused him to resent his wife. Make sure that doesn't happen to you.

A combination of separate and joint accounts is probably a great idea if your partner handles money significantly differently from you. But be forewarned, it is pretty complicated. To make this work, all income should go into a joint account/s, and all savings, debt, and retirement are managed jointly. Additionally, each individual has a private checking account into which a set amount is transferred each month. That "personal fund" can be spent on any wants and needs they have that aren't a joint expense, e.g., gifts, shoes on Amazon, etc. I have found this to be one of the best solutions for couples with different outlooks on money. If you go for this route, at least you won't get a heart attack when you log into your online joint account and see a $400 statement for headphones. Many couples like this because it gives more spending freedom on the agreed-upon money that goes into the personal funds after bills, savings, and retirement funds are sorted. The only caveat here is that you'll need to open and manage several bank accounts. And you also need to be okay with that monthly "allowance" that you agree on —assuming the term allowance doesn't offend you.

• **Can you live on one income and save the second?**

In today's society, where both individuals work for a living, two incomes create more financial stability in the home. With the arrival of the new baby, your wife will likely want to take as much time off as possible, even if it's unpaid leave. It would be a wise decision to discuss whether you can start living as though you only have one income for the next several months so you can save the second income. That would require that all your expenses and contributions fit into this single income so you can out the second income into short and long-term savings. Use automation to send the second income directly to a savings account, so you never even see it. Try this until the baby arrives and if you see the benefits out-weight the sacrifice, consider picking up this strategy once the new mommy resumes work. Feel free to customize it to fit your long-term goals. For example, you could save 100% of the second income until the baby arrives, after which you slash it to 50% that remains in perpetuity.

Don't overlook this - ensure you're financially prepared for a new family.

Just as necessary as regular date night to keep that flame of romance alive, you should also schedule finance night. Whether you'll keep everything separate and split the bills equally, share everything or divide it up into mine, yours, and ours, a regular sit-down is imperative. There's no one size fits all approach because the only thing that matters is you both agree and align with your chosen strategy.

SAVING AND SPENDING YOUR MONEY WISELY

You're a family man now. Congratulations! It's time to stop thinking and spending recklessly. Thanks to this new family, your money's value has exponentially increased because every dollar spent wisely adds to your baby's well-being and future happiness. It's time to start practicing smart personal finance, so you don't get overburdened with expenses. That doesn't mean depriving yourself or your wife in any way. If there's a need, you should always meet it. What it means is that you should think twice about buying the latest iPhone just because they tweaked a few things from their previous release. It also means that you don't need a new pair of those top-of-the-line tennis shoes when yours are still in good condition. I don't know what your thing is, but regardless of what you splurge on, it's time to think like a dad.

Decide what matters to you, set some financial goals, and start saving toward that. Keep your credit cards but decrease where and how you use them. Speaking of shopping for things, do you really need to be the most trendy guy in the office? It's time to leave that mantle to the young single guys. You don't need to pay a premium on stuff that goes out of style faster than Kardashians can shoot a reality show season. Instead, go for things that are quality and well priced. Let all your shopping trips be thoughtful and planned out, whether it's baby shopping or home shopping.

THE KEY TAKEAWAY FOR THIS CHAPTER:

- Babies are fantastic, but they come with a hefty price tag. That's why you and your wife need to get on the same page and align your finances.
- You must develop a family budget that you can start testing so that by the time the baby arrives, you won't experience the strain of additional expenses. Stick to whatever family budget works best. Commit and remain consistent.
- Be aware of the hidden hospital add-ons.

Create estimates for the baby's expenses before, during, and after birth.

- Figure out your financial situation, decide which strategy works for you based on the various options outlined in this chapter, and please make sure your debt is clear. Pay off whatever you can before the baby arrives.

- Use a budgeting app to track and manage all your expenses and be open to the conversation of surviving on a single income before the baby's arrival so you can give yourself a financial head start.

- Go easy on yourself and please make the topic of finances something enjoyable for both you and the Mrs.

Action plan:

Think of one small thing you can do today to move forward in your financial planning as a new dad. If you don't have an existing budget, that's a great starting point. Put together your first family budget. Remember, you need to work out what you spend now, then decide what to cut back, where to save and how to save.

5

PREGNANCY - YOUR WEEK-BY-WEEK GUIDE ON WHAT TO EXPECT AND HOW TO FULLY SUPPORT YOUR WIFE

We're at the heart of your adventure now. It's time to get specific about what you can expect during the pregnancy and how to maintain a sense of calm throughout. Your wife needs a helpful, loving partner. She needs someone to take care of her when the burden feels too much to bear. You need insights on how to become that man. Don't worry, none of us were born with the natural talent of being the best husband during this period. We simply learn (mainly through trial and error) what works and what doesn't. The best part about picking up this book is you get to have less guesswork and more insight going into this adventure. But don't be fooled; all the books in the world cannot cover or anticipate each and every experience over the coming months, so you'll still need to rely on the cultivated mindfulness that we learned about in chapter 1.

The most important thing is to get your mindset right and prioritize your wife's well-being and proper care throughout this pregnancy. Henceforth, every decision you make should consider her needs because when she's happy, you'll be less stressed, trust me.

The rest of this chapter focuses on the different stages the expectant mom will go through, what you should know about it, and some tips on being an involved partner.

Conception:

Conception took place when your wife's ovum (egg) finally got conquered by your sperm. The gender and inherited characteristics are decided in that instant. In other words, as you read this, regardless of how many weeks you are into the pregnancy, your baby's gender and characteristics are already determined.

THE FIRST TRIMESTER (1ST TO 3RD MONTH)

After fertilization and implantation, a baby is at first just an embryo: two layers of cells from which all the organs and body parts will develop.

The first three months of pregnancy are critical. Your baby is developing rapidly and is most at risk from hazardous substances like alcohol, drugs, or habits like smoking, etc. This is when it goes from that embryo to a formed fetus, and it's the period in which the organs will form and begin various functions. It's also the period where the risk of a miscarriage is the highest. As soon as you receive the news, decide on the best changes to ensure the health and well-being of the pregnancy and the mom-to-be. Let's break this down into a general week-by-week development but keep in mind that exact details for both mom and baby may vary.

Week 1:

The first week is actually your wife's menstrual period. Her expected birth date (EDD or EDB) is calculated from the first day of her last period and counts as part of the 40-week pregnancy even though conception hadn't occurred. Don't ask me why; I don't get it either, and I revert to an expert OBGYN to give a more scientific answer.

Week 2:

This is when fertilization of the egg by the sperm will take place. It's typically toward the end of this week.

Week 3:

Thirty hours after conception, the cell splits into two. Three days later, the cell, also called the zygote, divides itself into 16 cells. After two more days, the zygote migrates from the fallopian tubes to the uterus (womb) of your partner. Then seven days after conception, the zygote burrows itself into the plump uterine lining (endometrium). At this point, the zygote is renamed to blastocyst.

Week 4:

The developing baby is tinier than a grain of rice at this point. The cells rapidly divide and continue forming the various body systems, including the digestive system.

Week 5:

A neural tube evolves, eventually becoming the central nervous system, i.e., the brain and spinal cord. But we're still a long way from that. Let's not get ahead of ourselves.

Week 6:

The developing baby is now known as an embryo, and it is around 3 mm in length. At this stage of development, your embryo is secreting special hormones that prevent the mother from having a menstrual period.

Week 7:

And we have a heartbeat! That's right. Our tiny embryo has developed its very own placenta and amniotic sac. The placenta burrows into the uterine wall to access oxygen and nutrients directly from its mother's bloodstream.

Week 8:

The embryo is now about 1.3 cm in length. Talk about rapid growth. The spinal cord at this point looks more like a tail, and its head is disproportionately large.

Week 9:

The baby's eyes, mouth, and tongue are taking form. The tiny muscles allow the embryo to start moving about. The embryo's new liver is also busy at work making the much-needed blood cells.

Week 10:

At this stage of the embryo's development, it's upgrading into a fetus and is about 2.5 cm in length. It's pretty much a baby, just tiny and still weird-looking. All of the bodily organs are formed. The hands and feet, which previously looked like paddles, are now evolving fingers and toes. The brain is also active and has brain waves.

Week 11:

Teeth are now budding inside the gums of your baby, and the tiny heart is developing further into full form.

Week 12:

The fingers and toes are recognizable at this point, but they're still stuck together with webs of skin. This is often the time to take the first trimester combined screening test (maternal blood test + ultrasound of baby). This test is necessary as it checks for trisomy 18, aka Edward syndrome, and trisomy 21, aka Down syndrome. Ask your OBGYN or midwife to explain these terms further on your 12-week checkup.

Week 13:

At week thirteen, you're finally leaving the first trimester. Can you believe it? Congratulations to both you and your wife for making it this far. Your tiny fetus can swim about quite vigorously. It's now more than 7 cm in length. Vocal cords are starting to form, and that big baby head is getting more in balance with the rest of the body. At this point, though, the head is about half of the size of his entire frame. I think you're starting to see why some cartoons have big heads. Your little one looks more like an alien from outer space but don't worry, by the time you get to the last few weeks before delivery, everything will be just the right size.

As you can see, the baby's development is rapid and unceasing. It goes through various stages and names within the first twelve weeks until it finally becomes a fetus. By the time you cross over to the second trimester, your baby has gone from a grain of rice at month one to a human-like baby fetus that's almost 3 inches long!

WHAT'S GOING ON WITH YOUR WIFE:

- Body processes and hormones go into overdrive.
- Progesterone and estrogen production rise significantly.
- Mood swings become common.
- Morning sickness.
- Achy and tender breasts.
- Constipation.
- Morning sickness.

But it's not all doom and gloom because some women have very mild or no morning sickness. You'll also notice the glowing "pregnancy skin" going on due to increased blood flow.

HOW YOU CAN HELP:

Communication is vital. Let her know in every way possible that you are there for her and your unborn child. Be as supportive and optimistic as you can. I know that might be hard if you work a 12-hour shift or you have a long commute with traffic and a jerk for a boss. That's why your mindset is key to success.

Your new dad mindset will enable you to handle the pressures of life and still show up as the best expectant father your wife would ever ask for. Go back to the game plan we outlined in the previous chapter and take the initiative. Work on setting goals, creating a family budget, changing up the eating habits, etc. Encourage healthy eating, light exercising, lots of laughter, and just being in each other's company. Use this time to get more vulnerable and to discuss topics that will impact your future. Go through that inner child exercise and ensure you heal your emotions and leave behind any baggage that might threaten your family's happiness. This is the best time to get educated. Become curious about yourself and your wife. Learn about what's best for her to eat so you can produce the healthiest baby in the world. If you enjoy cooking, perhaps it's time to learn some new recipes so you can become her personal chef over the coming months. If you never bothered with housework, grocery shopping, and mundane tasks like these, it's time to step up and show her you're all in.

One last thing, don't forget to integrate your mindfulness practices so you can hold that optimism for both of you, especially when she's having a bad day. Brace yourself for lots of emotional outbursts as the hormones flair up.

THE SECOND TRIMESTER (4TH TO 6TH MONTH)

At the beginning of the second trimester, your baby is about 3.5 inches long and weighs about 1.5 ounces. The baby has tiny unique fingerprints, and the heart pumps 25 quarts of blood daily. At this point, the skeleton is still rubbery cartilage, but it will harden into bone within the next few weeks.

Week by week development:

Week 14:

It's fourteen weeks, and you're well into the second trimester, which is usually said to be the best trimester for an expectant couple. Your baby is measuring about three and a half and four inches long and weighing around 2 ounces (think of an orange or the size of your clenched fist). Although you and mom-to-be cannot feel it yet, that baby is constantly moving around like a little ballerina. The baby's neck is getting longer, which helps it stand more erect. The baby is also getting chubbier by the week, and some might even sprout some hair around the head and eyebrows. Other developments this week include more digestive system activity (intestines are producing meconium, a waste product you'll receive as her first bowel movement after birth. Just one of the many gifts you'll get for being a dad) and a roof inside the baby's mouth. The baby-to-be can also use facial muscles to grimace and smile at this point.

Week 15:

This week, your baby's skeleton starts to ossify, meaning it's taking visible form. Things are moving into place, and the fetus is looking more and more like a human baby. The eyes and ears slowly migrate to the rightful spots on the baby's face and head. Thank goodness.

Week 16:

This week your baby is making small side-to-side eye movements and can even perceive some light even though they are still closed for protection. By now, most baby's have picked up the sucking reflex, so yours is likely able to make sucking motions already. The little heart is also busy at work this week, pumping about 25 quarts of blood daily. Tiny bones in your fetus' ears are in place, making it likely that the baby will soon be able to pick up. Mommy's voice (or some version of it) within the next few weeks. Did you know that studies have found that babies who hear a song while in the womb can recognize the same tune when it's sung to them after they're born? How cool is that? It's time to get that baby playlist ready and switch on your home Karaoke sessions because you'll soon be able to sing to that baby.

Week 17:

This week, your baby's body fat begins to form, with fat stores developing under the baby's skin. That will provide energy and keep your little one warm and cute after birth. If you could hold your baby at this point, it would be about the size of your palm (about 5 inches in length), weighing five or more ounces. From this point on, baby fat will continue to accumulate until the baby's born and thereafter. The heartbeat rate is also starting to stabilize into a regular 140-150 beats per minute. Yes, that's a fast heartbeat (twice as fast as yours), but this is the standard for a healthy growing fetus at this stage.

The baby's also getting more practice sucking and swallowing (essential when it comes to feeding after birth), and that's not all. Fingerprints are forming. You know how we say everyone's fingerprint is unique? This is the week the magic of that unique formation takes place.

Week 18:

If you have boneless chicken breast this week, guess what? Your baby is about the same size. How cool is that? Anytime in the next few weeks, your wife will experience that first real kick, roll, twist, or punching in the womb. This week the art of the yawn has been mastered by your baby, along with hiccupping. If you're lucky, you might even catch a glimpse of that adorableness in your next ultrasound. Speaking of ultrasounds, you can expect to find out the gender on that next one because the fallopian tubes and uterus are now in the proper position if it's a girl, and the genitals may be visible if it's a boy.

The baby's nervous system matures rapidly this week. A network of nerves now covered with a substance called myelin that helps speed messages from nerve cell to nerve cell is forming more complex connections. And those in the brain are further developing into the ones that serve the senses of touch, taste, smell, sight, and hearing. That means your baby's hearing is now more acute than ever, making them more conscious of sounds that come from around their environment. What does that mean? If your wife hiccups, your baby can hear that.

Week 19:

This week your baby's just over six inches long, weighs over half a pound, and seems to be covered in some kind of waxy cheese. Say what? That's right. A cheesy-looking substance called vernix caseosa now covers your fetus' skin. It's greasy looking and may not sound so appealing, but it's there for a good reason. Vernix protects your baby's sensitive skin from the surrounding amniotic fluid so that the baby doesn't come out of the womb looking like an old wrinkled bag that mommy had soaked in a bathtub for nine months.

Week 20:

This is the midpoint of this journey is here! You and your wife ought to be very thrilled and proud of yourself. Within the next two weeks, you're going to do the lengthier scan where your doctor can tell you about the baby's gender because at this point, the baby's uterus is fully formed, and the vaginal canal is starting its development if you're having a girl. If it's a boy, then the testicles are about to descend. Where are they now? Still in the abdomen waiting for the scrotum to finish growing, so they'll have somewhere to go in a few weeks. How incredible is your wife's oven? All that is taking place right before your very eyes.

Week 21:

This week, something incredible is happening to your baby. They are developing their taste buds which means, whatever your wife eats, your baby will start tasting it too. From this week on, your fetus will be swallowing a bit of amniotic fluid on a daily basis not only for nutrition and hydration but also as a form of practice. That's how the baby will eventually survive once it's born because it will need to swallow and digest its food.

Something important to note here is whatever your wife eats will directly influence your newborn. Researchers have pointed out that babies exposed to particular tastes in utero via the amniotic fluid were more eager to eat foods with those same tastes after birth. So, watch the diet in the house and try as much as possible to enjoy those veggies with your wife if you want your little one to feel that same connection later on!

Week 22:

This week, your cutie pie is making sense of the world and can tell the difference between day and night (light and darkness). Things get pretty interesting from here on out. Take a flashlight and shine it on your wife's tummy to see if you'll excite the little one into movement.

You should also know that your little one's grip is pretty firm. She likes to practice with the umbilical cord (very resourceful) since there's nothing around. But don't worry, nature knows that, so the cord can handle it. The baby can also hear the voice, heartbeat, and the whoosh-whoosh of your's wife's blood as it circulates.

Week 23:

This week your baby is just over a pound in weight and measures 11 inches long. Your baby's organs and bones have taken shape, but they are still visible through the skin, which seems to be a bit saggy since skin grows faster than fat. But soon, all that will change as the baby fat starts to fill things out pre-birth. The skin will also become less transparent as those fat deposits settle in. The baby punches will be more pronounced this week, and you might even see them poke from the outside if you're spending time hanging out with mommy's belly.

Week 24:

If you had a baby cam inside there, this might be the week you could almost tell what your baby's face will be. I mean, it's still a tiny face, but you could definitely see the definitive features because everything is almost fully formed. You have eyelashes, eyebrows, and hair. Wondering what hair color your baby is rocking? Actually, there's no pigment yet, so it's mostly just white. And there's also very little fat, so your baby, while beautiful, is still pretty transparent. You can see right through to all the bones, blood vessels, and organs. Pretty cool, right?

That's not all. He or she can now hear you! Yes, daddy, welcome to the picture. This is the week where the baby learns your voice, especially if you are daily engaging in some kind of direct play and activity with mommy and developing baby. So what are you waiting for? Go, sing, read, laugh, and talk to that beautiful belly!

Week 25:

This week the baby's lungs are gearing up to breathe, and so are your baby's nostrils. Of course, since there won't be any air for many more weeks, the baby will inhale amniotic fluid first, but that's okay. It's the practice that counts. Researchers also suspect that once the nose is activated, the baby could smell various scents in the utero, but even if that doesn't happen this week, it will kick in by the third trimester.

Week 26:

The baby now weighs a total of 2 pounds and measures about 14 inches long. Wow! That space is about to get pretty small, don't you think? Although now it's fun and easy to jump around and do somersaults, things will get a little cramped soon enough. After all these weeks, those little eyes finally opened. And although this is a pretty exciting thing to happen, the view is rather mundane, wouldn't you agree? So try this with your wife just for kicks. Shine that flashlight at the belly as often as you can and see if the baby responds.

This week you also have a lot of brain-wave activity, meaning your little one can not only hear noises but can now also respond to them.

Week 27:

It's the last week of your second trimester, and the baby is about 14.5 inches and around 2 pounds in weight. That's double what it was a mere four weeks ago. If you've been active, then your baby should now easily recognize both you and your wife's voices. Keep reading and singing to that belly because it's working. The baby taste buds are also very developed, so if your wife suddenly had a spicy meal, the baby would taste the difference immediately. Some babies respond to that spicy kick by hiccupping (your wife will pick this up in the form of belly spasms). Don't worry about baby hiccups. They are pretty normal and not distressing at all to the baby.

WHAT'S GOING ON WITH YOUR WIFE:

- Back pain and body aches become more frequent.
- She may experience discomfort in muscles and joints.
- Her hips and pelvis might feel a little sore from time to time, especially from week 18 when the hormone relaxin gets released to loosen the ligaments that hold her bones together.
- You might notice melasma. These are brown or gray patches that show up around the face.
- Larger and more protruding abdomen as the pregnancy becomes pronounced.
- Heartburn may occur in some pregnant women.
- At times, she might experience lightheadedness due to lower blood pressure.
- Appetite increase for most women.
- Snoring. If your wife didn't snore pre-pregnancy, don't worry, this should pass soon, but for now, try putting a humidifier in your

bedroom or just buy some earplugs and let her get some rest.

- Some women also experience swelling of the ankles or hands.

Your wife's body is undergoing rapid physical changes as the uterus grows and the belly's skin stretches to make room for the growing baby. Her breasts may also increase in size, and some women even develop stretchmarks around these areas, which may or may not fade over time. Toward the end of the second trimester, your wife will begin to notice baby movements and the sleeping and waking cycle that the unborn baby has formed.

HOW YOU CAN HELP:

This is generally considered the honeymoon period of pregnancy because most women lose their first trimester's headaches, nausea, and icky feelings. Although the baby is growing, it's not yet too big to create massive discomfort for your wife. So take advantage of her energy and do your best to fuel her optimism.

Start encouraging your pregnant wife to decide on things like when she would like to take her to leave from work and when she'll want to return if all goes according to plan? Find out her thoughts regarding her current job or career and whether she sees that changing once the baby is born.

It's also a great time to help your wife adopt healthy eating and still get in some light exercise. If she's experiencing aches and muscle tension, encourage her to stretch frequently to prevent sciatica. Making it a combined effort will help a lot. But don't overdo the workouts and stretches. Remember, her growing uterus is creating a lot of pressure on her ligaments and organs, so take it easy. Equally as important as being active and stretching is making sure she spends time off her feet. You can also consider getting her a belly band for a little extra support, especially if she's carrying twins.

If she gets late-night cravings and you need to drive around the neighborhood looking for a late-night grocery, then so be it. Do it with a smile. Consider adding high calcium foods into your current diet, as calcium is pretty vital for a pregnant woman. If milk and other dairy products aren't her things, you could go for sesame seeds, almonds, soy, tofu, and leafy green vegetables. Iron is another important addition you'll need to shop for. Iron-rich foods include beans, oat bran, barley, spinach, seaweed, pumpkin seeds, and meat.

Experiment and find what her appetite and hormones can tolerate.

Participate as much as you can in the baby planning activities even if you don't consider them to be "manly." I planned all three of my baby showers to surprise my wife. Of course, I had a little (a lot) of help from her best friend, but still, I loved the experience and the happy look on her face. Remember, this isn't just her pregnancy and baby; it's yours too. Get out of your comfort zone and do things you'd never thought about - like getting matching T-shirts at the baby shower that said, "we're pregnant and glowing!"

Your job during this trimester is to facilitate comfort, ease, and reassurance. If your wife is into massages, consider surprising her with a spa weekend. Does she enjoy the great outdoors? Look for fun experiences you can still enjoy together to ease her mind.

THE THIRD TRIMESTER (7TH TO 9TH MONTH)

Most babies will weigh about two and a quarter pounds by the start of the third trimester. They can blink their eyes and might even spot some eyelashes, and their wrinkly skin is starting to smoothen out as they put on baby fat.

They are also developing fingernails, toenails, and real hair (if we can call it that) while simultaneously adding billions of neurons to their brain. Yes, your baby is incredibly productive and working hard to get to the finish line. Most babies tend to weigh around 7 pounds by the time they are born. Did you know that the baby can see the light filtering in through the mother's womb in the third trimester?

Week by week development:

Week 28:

Welcome to the last lap, dad. You and your wife only have two more months to go, and this pregnancy experience will be over. This week your baby begins to experience REM (rapid eye movement(sleep, which could mean your little one is dreaming. So far, your baby's eyes have been shut tight. Now they can open and close to their heart's content, and these eyes come with brand new fluttering eyelashes. In the real world, the skill of blinking will become very useful as it helps keep out unwanted foreign materials. By now, your baby is about 15 inches long when measured head to toe and weighs almost 21/4 pounds. From this week on, the baby will start prepping for the grand exit by settling into the proper position for birth, all the while continuing to master skills like coughing, sucking, hiccupping, and perhaps most important, better breathing.

Week 29:

This week your baby starts to feel cramped in as the space gets smaller and smaller with every passing week. At this point, your wife should start doing daily kick counts once or twice a day (depending on what the doctor or midwife recommends), so you can monitor the baby. If you notice any changes in frequency, be sure to get in touch with your practitioner. It's easy to experience those kicks, jabs, and pokes mostly because there's less space, and the baby's getting stronger, less erratic, and more excited by all the stimuli he or she experiences. Movement, sound, light, and that sweet smoothie your wife loves all excite the baby. The baby is getting more fat, and the wrinkles are becoming less visible. Most babies will weigh between two and a half and three pounds at this point, but this number will likely double over the next 11 weeks.

Week 30:

This week brings lots of significant changes for the growing baby. For starters, your baby's bone marrow has completely taken over the production of red blood cells. Before this shift, tissue groups and the spleen took care of this task. Why is this a big deal? It ensures the baby will be able to thrive on her own after delivery takes place.

The baby's brain is also growing rapidly. Until now, the surface was smooth, but now, your fetus' brain is taking on those characteristic grooves and indentations. Those wrinkles allow for an increased amount of brain tissue which is necessary as your baby prepares to develop street smarts for life outside the womb.

Remember that soft, downy hair that has been covering your little one's body till this point? Well, no need for that furry coat anymore. Now that the baby's brain and new fat cells regulate body temperature, the lanugo's service is no longer needed. You might see a bit of left-over fur on your newborn's back and shoulders after the birth, but for the most part, it should be gone.

Week 31:

You'll be fascinated to learn that this week, your brainy baby can already process information and pick up signals from all five senses. That brain is working over-time these days, and it wouldn't be an understatement to say you've got a genius in the house because connections between individual nerve cells are being made at a super-fast rate. All this takes up a lot of energy, as you might imagine, which causes the baby to sleep a lot.

Your wife can probably tell when the baby is awake and when it is sleeping.

Week 32:

All major organs are fully developed now, except for the lungs. This week your baby's transparent skin is also changing into something more opaque. Suppose your wife suddenly needed an emergency delivery this week. In that case, there's a very high chance that both mommy and baby would be just fine because although the lungs aren't fully developed, your baby has been practicing using them. At this point, your baby looks pretty much like a newborn. At some point between weeks 32-38, the baby will probably settle into the head-down, bottoms-up presentation in your wife's pelvis in preparation for birth. Curious to know why they chose this position? According to experts, the fetus' head fits better at the bottom of a woman's inverted, pear-shaped uterus. Besides, it makes things easier during delivery if the baby's head pops out first. While some women do have what's medically termed a breech birth (bottom-down position), the numbers are pretty low (less than 5%), so don't worry too much if the doctor says the baby hasn't turned yet. Sometimes they wait till the last possible moment to flip.

What is else the baby doing this week in preparation for the big day? Honing the skills of swallowing, sucking, breathing, and more.

Week 33:

With only one more month left, your baby has reached the length he or she will measure at birth. Each week now, the baby is adding on about half a pound. Your wife might notice sharper kicks and shortness of breath because the baby has really outgrown the living space and is now crowing around your wife's lungs. If you had a baby cam in the uterus, here's what you'd see: Your fetus is acting more like a newborn with eyes closing during sleep and opening while awake. There's more baby than amniotic fluid, so your wife will experience sharper movement, and the baby can easily differentiate between day and night since those uterine walls are becoming thinner.

This week a huge milestone has been reached. Your baby has the immune system up and running. Antibodies are being passed from your wife to your little one as he or she continues to develop the immune system. That's one of the ways the baby will fend off all sorts of germs after delivery. And this is also why the home and all the baby spaces should be kept clean because the baby's immune system won't be that strong for a while.

Week 34:

This week something epic is happening, especially if your baby is a boy. Now is the time for testicles to make their way down from the abdomen to the scrotum. Some full-term baby boys (3% or so) are born with undescended testicles, but they usually make the trip down sometime before the first birthday. About 30% of preterm boys are born with undescended testicles too. In other baby-related developments, boy or girl, your little one's vernix is thickening this week, so it can start shedding soon. If you're spending enough time with mommy and her belly, you might spot body parts like little hands and feet poking through the belly!

Week 35:

This week your baby is standing tall at about 18 inches and weighs almost 51/4 pounds. Your baby's skinny arms and legs are now quite plump and irresistibly, squeezably soft.

Week 36:

This week your baby's ears are extra sharp, and that little body is getting chubbier by the minute. If this is your wife's first birth, you might notice a massive shift in the belly position as the baby drops lower into her pelvis. This is normal and is called lightening or drop-ping, and that might trigger a new walking style commonly known as the penguin waddle. The good news about "dropping" is that it will enable your wife to take deeper breaths and eat more comfortably.

At 36 weeks, your baby's skull bones are not fused yet, so the head can quickly (well, relatively easily) maneuver through the birth canal. Most of her bones and cartilage are quite soft, allowing for an easier journey into the world during delivery. Over the first few years, all the bone structures will harden.

Week 37:

This week your baby continues practicing and rehearsing for the big day, simulating breathing by inhaling and exhaling amniotic fluid, sucking the tiny thumb, blinking, and pivoting from side to side. It's become super crowded in the uterus, so the baby won't kick as much. Instead, your baby will stretch, roll and do a bit of wiggling, all of which your wife will be able to feel. The baby's head continues to grow this week and will, in fact, remain pretty huge compared to the rest of the body.

Week 38:

All systems are going this week, and as you and mom-to-be prepare for last-minute stuff, so is your baby. This week, your little one continues to shed vernix and lanugo. He or she is also swallowing amniotic fluid, which winds up in her intestines where it and other shed cells, bile, and waste products will turn into the baby's first bowel movement, aka meconium. Hello, first diaper change.

This week the lungs continue to mature and produce more and more surfactant, a substance that prevents the air sacs in the lungs from sticking to each other once she's out in the world and breathing our air.

Week 39:

Congratulations daddy! You and mom-to-be are now at full term. And while the baby's body isn't growing as much, the brain is still on overdrive activity. It's already 30% bigger than it was just four weeks ago. Your baby's pinkish skin has turned whitish or whitish gray and won't have pigmentation no matter what the final skin color will be. A pigmentation is an after-the-birth event. Your baby now weighs around 7 to 8 pounds and measures 19 to 21 inches. Knowing that your wife can go any day, you should be watching out for signs of labor. These include water breaking, diarrhea, or nausea which many women experience just before the onset of labor; spurts of energy, aka the nesting instinct; the loss of the mucus plug (the cork of mucus that seals the opening of the uterus); bloody show which arrives when the woman's capillaries rupture from the dilation and effacement of her cervix causing any discharge to appear pink or red-tinged.

Week 40:

Welcome to the official end of your pregnancy. If the baby doesn't come this week, don't worry; you're not alone. An estimated 30% of pregnancies proceed past the 40-week mark. Talk to your baby and wife a lot and give plenty of encouragement. Your wife is continuing with the job of providing the antibodies the baby will need to fight off infections for the first six months of her life. And the baby will complete shedding most of the vernix that was acting as a moisturizer. At this point, some dry spots may appear on the skin after birth. Stay alert for any labor signs and talk to your health provider about when, why, and how you might induce your wife into labor if that's something you're both comfortable with. Most doctors will induce around week 41.

If you're thinking about home birth, this might be the time to sure up that backup plan in case medical assistance becomes necessary.

Week 41:

Still going strong, your baby might be cramped in there, but all is going well. Your baby's nails will need a manicure and pedicure as they've now grown well past the fingertips. Make sure you have baby nail clippers waiting at home. Don't worry too much about being overdue. In fact, you're not considered overdue until 42 weeks gestation. Less than 5% of babies arrive on their due date. Your count was likely a little of, nothing to stress about. For now, continue to monitor the baby's heartbeat through a non-stress test. Make sure the heart rate quickens each time he or she moves. Focus on your wife and make sure she doesn't stress over the due date. This is the time to experiment with those relaxation techniques that you learned in prenatal classes.

Week 42:

At this point, the doctor is going to recommend you induce labor to assist with the process. Since there's a chance your wife's placenta may not provide as much oxygen and nutrients to your baby, the doctor will suggest the safest way to get the baby out. If you've been planning a home birth, your midwife might suggest breaking your wife's water. This is a very common option, and it works for many women. Some just need that little extra help, and the contractions initiate almost instantly.

Mom and baby will be receiving extra attention this week, and that's a good thing. Although most babies continue to thrive well past week 40, your doctor will frequently monitor the baby with a biophysical profile - an ultrasound to assess the baby plus a non-stress test. When this latecomer finally makes its debut, chances are the baby's skin will be dry, cracked, peeling, or wrinkled. These are all completely temporary, so don't worry about it. The good news is, your baby will be super alert and relieved it's finally over as well. The most important thing this week is to remain calm and supportive of your wife. If you panic, she will, too, and she's already having a terrible time feeling like she's been pregnant forever. So you need to keep stress in the home at a minimum. Treat her special all week and find ways to keep her optimistic. Your little bundle is almost here, and everything will work out in the end!

WHAT'S GOING ON WITH YOUR WIFE:

- Plenty of physical discomfort as the weight of her growing baby starts to take its toll on her.
- Backaches are a daily complaint.
- Shortness of breath.
- Lots and lots of heartburn.
- Some women will develop spider veins, varicose veins, and hemorrhoids due to increased blood circulation.
- Frequent urination as the baby moves deeper into her pelvis.

- Braxton Hicks contractions might occur. These are irregular contractions that your wife will feel, like a slight tightness in her abdomen. They are more likely to happen in the afternoon or evening or even after physical activity like sex. If she's close to her due date, she might also experience them but call your doctor if there's increased intensity and frequency.
- Emotionally, your wife is getting anxious about the childbirth process, and she might be worried about how long it will last and whether everything will go according to plan.

HOW YOU CAN HELP:

- Make sure you're accompanying her for every checkup, so she doesn't feel abandoned by his burden.
- Don't be afraid to show off your massage skills, especially when her back or feet become unbearable.
- Become a great listener. Most of the time, it will be enough to just sit with her and listen to her anguish and emotional meltdowns if they do occur. At this point, complaints aren't to torture you but rather to feel heard. If you can tell and

show her how much you appreciate her work in carrying this baby, that will make all the difference in her world.

- Get creative and find new ways of making her comfortable. If her feet are swollen, encourage her to elevate her legs frequently and perhaps increase fiber intake. If she's struggling with heartburn, start cooking and packing foods in smaller portions so she can eat frequently but in smaller quantities. This is also a great time to hide away the frier and when you go grocery shopping, avoid getting spicy food or citrus fruits. And no matter what she tells you, chocolate only makes things worse for someone prone to heartburn. Keep it away from the house.

THE KEY TAKEAWAY FOR THIS CHAPTER:

- Pregnancy is an adventure that begins with the first trimester being a little bumpy (or a lot) then switches into the honeymoon period before finally hitting the last stretch, which is usually dreadful for your wife.
- Your role is to be there for your wife at each stage. Be the calm, reassuring, helpful, and loving partner she needs. Take care of her and

be willing to go the extra mile, even if it means learning to do the dishes and taking out the trash. Does she love massages? Great. It's time for you to turn those sausage hands into magical performers.

- Be as involved as you'd like to be. That doesn't mean you should neglect your own well-being. Instead, it means you will need to take care of yourself even more so you always have enough mental and emotional stamina to support your wife.

- Sing and talk to your baby as the belly grows. It's hard to imagine this, but your unborn child is extremely active and sensitive to sights and sounds. The more proactive you are with mom and baby, the more connected they will feel to you and vice versa.

Action plan:

It's time to wear your new dad hat and start implementing what you've learned in this chapter. How many weeks or months is your pregnant wife? Based on the information you've learned, what should you be expecting and doing for her? Consider everything from her current diet, emotional state, physical exercise, aches, and pains. What's one thing you could do today that would show her how loving and supportive you are as an expectant dad?

Remember, your job is to support her to have a safe, smooth, and relatively pain-free pregnancy. Part of that is getting ahead of the childbirth process and weighing the best options for mom, baby, and your finances. Let's do that next.

6

HOME, HOSPITAL, OR CLINIC CHILDBIRTH? WHICH IS MORE SUITABLE FOR YOU AND YOUR WIFE?

W ondering what options will be safest for your wife and unborn child during the delivery process? You're not alone. Although most births occur in hospitals, this is a relatively new shift that has become the norm since the mid 20th century. Before that, most mothers had babies at home.

Although many are turning back to home births, it's wise to educate yourself on the pros and cons so you and your wife can make an informed decision. I also encourage you to have this conversation with your doctor once the prenatal visits start.

DOES IT MAKE SENSE TO GO FOR A HOSPITAL BIRTH OR NOT?

The Harvard Health Publication reports that roughly 15% of women planning a home birth will require transfer to the hospital. It also states that there are no national standards for integrating home birth into a continuum of care in the U.S. There are no agreed-upon criteria to help identify good candidates for home birth, nor are there standards to ensure adequate training of those attending home births.

So basically, you're on your own if you opt for a home birth. But don't let that discourage you (especially if your personal preference is such) because there's not enough data that verifies whether or not home births are a risker. If anything, the little data that exists seems to show that most of the time, a home birth only becomes dangerous if the mother wasn't necessarily healthy. But even then, the mortality rate isn't significantly higher than hospital births. With that said, you'll need to make a decision. So let's look at some of the pros and cons of each available option.

A personal share:

My wife and I had our first birth at home, and while we did have some unexpected issues that came up resulting in a hospital transfer, the overall experience was worthwhile. The hospital visit was short and not too much of an emergency. With our second child, we decided to give the hospital birth a chance, but the experience turned out less pleasant than expected, and so for our third birth, we went back to having a home birth with our trusted midwife and doula. Both home births were incredible experiences for me as a dad, and I know some men are pretty scared about the child delivery process, but it's not as messy as your imagination wants you to believe. In fact, for many dads that I know, doing it that natural way and being present for the entire experience was incredible and it helped strengthen their connection to both their wife and newborn. I don't know your personality or preference, but I encourage you to explore this path as a possibility.

PROS AND CONS OF HOSPITAL BIRTH

Hospital birth is an excellent option for women who have a high-risk pregnancy or women who prefer the maternity ward to a room at home.

For the pros - this option is considered the safest because you have all the medical support possible if something goes wrong. If, during the labor process, things turn for the worst and the doctor deems it necessary to perform a C-section, there'll be no time wasted.

You also have the luxury of experienced staff, advanced medical technology, anesthesiologists to help your wife with labor pains, and immediate medical care if the baby needs it upon arrival.

For the cons - I think we can all agree hospitals are expensive even if you have insurance coverage. The bigger the hospital, the more impersonal it will be, and sometimes that can be pretty stressful for you and your wife.

If you're considering a big hospital, you might want to go for a few tours to familiarize yourself with the place. You should also be okay with the fact that your wife and child will have no privacy whatsoever. Doctors and nurses will come and go as they please, and don't even think you'll get any rest during this process.

Once the baby is born, the standard protocol is for the newborn to be separated from the mother. If you want your baby with you at all times, this may not be possible in most hospitals. Although many hospitals now offer premium services and more customized experiences, it comes at a cost and has many limitations. As a hospital, the caregivers must follow standard procedures and protocols, so you probably want to consider a different alternative like home birth if you're not big on mass regulations.

PROS AND CONS OF HOME BIRTH

For the pros - you have more control over the entire experience. The labor process and delivery occur in a familiar setting for the mother, which can be a source of strength and calmness.

If you happen to follow certain strict religious or cultural beliefs, they can be taken to account and adhered to. There's also no pressure to use medications or interventions, which many obstetricians agree is a good thing. Your delivery cost is significantly lowered, and if you happen to have a short labor experience, the process can be over pretty fast.

One thing I've heard women praise about this option is the fact that they were at liberty to choose their most preferred labor positions and other elements of the birthing process. That's not an option. they get in a hospital because the authorities determine what position she has to stay in, whether she can eat, drink, etc.

At home, it's a different story. Your wife gets to play boss, and she receives whatever V.I.P treatment she desires. She decides what she wants to do. Does she want candles all over the place? Would she like a warm bath or shower or some aromatherapy during labor? You can arrange anything she desires, and with the guidance of the doula and midwife, she can have her dream experience all in the comfort of your home. That was a very appealing option for my wife, and since her pregnancies were all low-risk, it was possible to make her dream a reality.

For the cons - we need to consider that even with your newly established health insurance, they may not cover any associated costs. If you're a stickler for medical technologies and interventions being at hand, this may not be possible at home. Your midwife certainly has the basic medical devices needed to monitor mom and baby during labor, although it's not as extensive as you'd find in a hospital. That's why people who don't like medical interventions generally go for this option. But you will get the basics like temperature, blood pressure, pulse, and the baby's heart rate taken care of.

In the event of an emergency, you'll need a fast way to get to the hospital, so you might want to think about the logistics of that. A big thing that scares the crap out of new dads is the "scenery." Homebirths are messy— way messier than hospital birth. So not only do you need to consider purchasing the right kind of sheets and towels and prep the room, but you should also think about whether or not you can handle the labor, delivery, and post-delivery experience. This varies from person to person, but as I shared earlier, it's not as scary or as messy as you might be thinking.

Wondering what that home birth shopping list might look like? Here are some of the things you'll need. A peri bottle, bulb syringe, Hibiclens, an antiseptic soap, cord clamps, sterile gloves, lubricant, alcohol prep pads, a variety of gauze pads, and postpartum use absorbent pads with a waterproof bottom. Of course, there are more things you could get, so get the complete list from your midwife and doctor.

If you feel a home birth is right for you, create a birth plan with your midwife's (and OBGYN's) approval and make sure she advises you on the necessary steps to make, this happens at home. But if after reading this, you're thinking, "there has to be something better than a hospital but not as daunting as the home birth." And you're right. Read on for my third alternative.

PROS AND CONS OF A BIRTHING CENTER

A birthing center is a homey, low-tech birthing option for expectant parents who don't like the hospital experience but aren't quite ready to do a full home-birth experience. In a birth center, midwives (not OBGYNs) are the primary care providers. Birthing centers can be standalone facilities, but more often than not, they tend to be adjacent to or inside a hospital.

For pros - we have to acknowledge that a birthing center is perhaps one of the more comfortable options you can find. Birth centers usually have soft lighting, a queen or double bed, a television, a rocking chair, couches for family and friends, a shower, a jacuzzi tub, and sometimes a kitchen. In many facilities, families are encouraged to personalize the room by hanging pictures, lighting candles, and putting on soothing music. And when it comes to privacy, it doesn't get any better than this. Unlike a standard hospital, you'll get a private room in a birthing center. That also means you and your wife have the freedom to be as active as you like. She can wear what she wants, move around as she wants, and even eat a light meal or snack during and after labor if she's up to it. A birthing center also allows mommy and baby to stay in the same room. Unlike with a hospital delivery where your baby is taken to a different room for first checkups and a few other procedures, you get to keep your baby with you all the time in a birthing center. It's also a shorter stay because recovery tends to be quicker due to fewer medications and medical interventions. The typical stay time is between four and eight hours after birth. That means you get to spend less money. And if you're wondering, the norm is for hospitals is usually between 24 to 48 hours.

For cons - we should probably mention that birthing centers aren't always readily available in every town, so if you happen to live in a small town, you might need to travel a great distance to find one. If you run into an emergency or problem labor, you'll be transferred to a hospital which, of course, creates further complications financially. Fortunately, that's not a very common occurrence. Data shows that less than 2% of transfers are due to emergencies. Another thing to consider before getting excited about this option is that your insurance might not cover this type of birth. So the first thing you must do is call your insurance broker to discuss your coverage. And if you're not thrilled about a birthing center, that's okay. It's not a solution that's ideal for every couple. If you're worried your wife is having a high-risk pregnancy, then perhaps this wouldn't be the right choice anyway. Birthing centers aren't equipped for difficult births. If your wife has a history of diabetes, hypertension, or anything that might complicate delivery, you might want to consider a hospital option. And although the birthing center is cheaper than a hospital, it still costs money. Typically between $3000 and $4000, so you still need to consider your finances before making this decision.

THE KEY TAKEAWAY FOR THIS CHAPTER:

- There is no one-size-fits-all answer for childbirth options. Whether you choose to have a home birth, hospital birth, or book a birthing center depends on your finances, lifestyle, and personal preference.
- Before deciding on which option to settle for, discuss it with your wife, healthcare provider, and your insurance broker to gain exact knowledge on what's covered.
- Some couples prefer to have the presence of medical backup in case of unforeseen complications, even if they have a low-risk pregnancy. Having highly trained professionals at their beck and call seems to be reassuring. Other couples value privacy and a personalized touch over high-tech facilities and medical interventions. These are the couples likely to opt for a birthing center. And some couples want everything to be *au naturel* so staying at home and saving on the hospital costs is their better option. You get to make that decision for your family.
- Child labor is messy no matter which option you choose, but yes, a home birth will be more gruesome than others. So it's time to man up

and get mentally fit because even if you get lightheaded, nauseous, and maybe even pass out, your wife will still need you to be there in that critical hour. You can do this!

Action plan:

Have you and your wife already decided on your child-birth option? If not, this is the time to engage her in this important discussion. When choosing, be mindful of your situation. Think about your location, financial resources, what the doctor advised, and the current health of your wife. Does she have a high-risk or a low-risk pregnancy? Let these factors guide your decisions so you can balance preference and personal convictions with pragmatic risk management.

Above all else, ensure both you and mom-to-be feel confident about the final choice.

7

PREPARING FOR THE BIG DAY

By now, you should be feeling a little more in control of the things that would otherwise drive you insane. Things like budget projections over the coming weeks and months, where and how the baby will be born, what your insurance will cover, and so on. With the help of your professional health provider, I expect you and your wife have settled on the best childbirth option. With that big decision out of the way, it's time to gear up both mentally and physically. You're heading toward the home stretch, so it's time to ensure you've prepared a welcoming environment for your baby both mentally and physically. Now is also a great time to help your wife prep the birth bag or the room (if you've opted for a home birth). In this chapter, we discuss the various things to prep for regardless of your chosen path. But before we get to that, let's talk about the basic things you and your wife need to do irrespective of the birthing option.

THE ESSENTIALS

• Build up your life toolbox

One of the most important things you can do to gear up for fatherhood is to develop a self-care plan and to acquire as many life tools as possible that you can start using as the family dynamics change. There are specific mental exercises (think of them like tools and techniques) that you can use to train your brain to accept and even like change, and here are the top-recommended ones.

#1: Learn to meditate.

Going back to our mindfulness practice, if you can invest some time daily (as little as 10minutes) to practice mindfulness through meditation, you'll better handle stress, change, and the challenges of fatherhood.

#2: Turn those negatives into positive tools.

This one isn't always easy to do, but you can turn any negative story into a positive or at least a neutral with a bit of practice. And that makes all the difference when in the midst of chaos. If you catch yourself thinking or saying, "this is bad," pause, take a deep breath, and turn that thought around by saying, "what if it's not all bad? Could it maybe be good?"

#3: Daily gratitude.

Each day, observe and identify three things you can be thankful for, no matter how small. This is especially helpful when things are challenging, and stress is high as you adjust to the new family setup. Didn't get much sleep because of the baby last night? Yes, that is hard, but rather than go into work grumpy, notice how good that office coffee and those finder sandwiches taste. Be grateful that your co-worker surprised you by getting a head start on your proposal, so you didn't have so much work to do. Notice how the traffic seemed to cut you some slack or anything else that's working for you that day. Instead of dwelling on the dull and negative side of life, get into the habit of picking just three positives in your day and train your brain to

#4: Never compare notes with friends. Instead, you must follow your gut.

I am all for creating a support structure for fellow dads or new parents so you can swap stories about this unique season in your life. Finding your tribe will make you feel like you're not alone, especially as you adjust to this family life. It also makes it easier to get recommendations of meal planning ideas, great babysitters, hot baby stuff deals, and more. However, if you have created such a support structure, know where to draw the line.

If you have friends with children, you need to fight the urge of assuming your pregnancy, delivery, and first few months of your baby's life "should be to be a certain way," okay? No baby comes with a manual, and no two children are alike in their journey.

Maybe your friend tells you that labor is supposed to be short/long/easy/ hard etc. or that newborns never cry/always cry. These are all experiences based on your friend's perspective and have nothing to do with what you'll experience. If his wife didn't want to have sex with him for a year after the baby was born and that killed their intimacy, it doesn't mean your wife will be the same. She might be all over you before her six-week checkup. Who knows? The point is, if you don't want to drive yourself mad wondering what's wrong with your life, do not compare it to anyone else. Your family is unique, and so are you. Everything depends on you holding this perspective.

#5: Take regular mindful walks.

Taking mindful walks even around the neighborhood or local park is a wonderful way to clear your head, ground yourself and refocus on your long-term goals and visions. Some dads do this with their little infants when it's their turn to watch the baby. Many dads report that taking their babies out for some fresh air tends to ease them into sleep, especially when they're a little older.

• **Create your baby zones**

That new arrival is tiny in size but trust me, he or she will quickly take over every square inch of your house if you don't designate specific areas wholly devoted to your noisy cherub. One way to do this is to set up a changing zone in one room of your house. If you have a big house, then you could have two areas - one on every floor.

The changing zone is where all the messy poo stuff happens, and it's where you can always find the organized diaper bag. That might help minimize the upcoming poo fragrance, and it ensures the house remains somewhat orderly.

In addition to this, consider setting feeding zones, sleeping zones, play zones, and any other zone you think the baby will need. I recommend having a little breastfeeding basket or tray set up next to where the new mom plans to hang out regularly. Ensure that basket has lots of bibs, a nursing pillow, hand sanitizer, pacifier, wipes, burp cloths, tissues, chocolate (yes, she can have some chocolate now), and anything else the baby and mommy might need so she can avoid running around when the baby starts demanding food especially in the middle of the night.

Fair warning, this doesn't eliminate the tiny socks and colorful chunks of playthings that you'll be stubbing your toe against in the middle of the night as you make zombie bathroom rounds. Still, it will keep them to a minimum, giving you a sense of control over your house. If you don't do this, you might walk into the house one day and wonder what happened to the man of the house.

• Double check your baby zones have all essential supplies

Now that you have specific zones for the baby to change, feed, play, etc., you want to ensure the necessary supplies are always there. It's a good idea to only purchase what you know the baby will use in the first three months of their life. Don't overdo this. Here's a list of must-haves to stock up on.

- Diapers, baby wipes, and diaper sacks (you can use nappies if that's the plan but regardless, get as much as you can).
- Changing mat.

- Soft baby towels.
- Baby bath or bath support.
- Non-biological detergent.
- Baby cot.
- Blankets.
- Formula milk and/or breast pump.
- Bottles.
- Bibs.
- Bottle sterilizer.

• Pick a pediatrician

One dreadful night, while half asleep, you might be forced to figure out a way to reach a pediatrician to help with the baby because it's making weird sounds while sleeping or having a high fever, and your wife is in total panic mode. When that happens, you'll be glad you already shortlisted a handful of pediatricians who came highly recommended and offered a reasonable price for in-house visits or late-night calls. If you live far from a big hospital or don't like hospitals, this is especially important. Start asking other parents in your area or do some online research. Next, make an appointment to visit a handful of your favorites. After interviewing them, pick one as your primary doctor but have a backup in the case on the day you need to take the baby; he or she isn't available.

• Set up a baby nursery

Have you agreed on where the baby will sleep? Great. Start making some room for the new arrival. If a nursery is part of your plan and budget, decorate the room, organize for those necessary furniture pieces and add the cozy final touches before the baby's arrival.

Giving your baby their own little space, even if it's at the corner of your bedroom, really makes a difference and acknowledges that you've gone from two to three members of the family. If you can start researching online for great deals on baby furniture in the second trimester, you can have this done by the third with plenty of time to spare for other more critical things. I would recommend setting up the nursery two months before the baby's due date. If you have a separate room for the baby, make sure it's not too far. Also, don't go too crazy with those baby decorations. Opt for warm, calming colors and a minimalist look to ease the baby into this new environment. If your wife is into Feng Shui, you could get a book to help you arrange the baby room in the most appropriate way.

• Do some low-level baby proofing

I know it might seem too early to do this because the baby isn't born but trust me, better to start early. Once the baby comes, both you and your wife will be so busy you'll likely procrastinate. At least get the most dangerous area's baby proofed and then add to that as the baby grows. A good starting point is to install some electrical cord management and plug covers. Don't go crazy here. After all, that baby won't be mobile for the first six months, so you have time.

• Choose a baby name

Although you can choose your baby's name whenever you like including after the arrival, many parents like to do it in advance. Perhaps you and your wife can start discussing different alternatives and shortlist your favorites, then wait until the baby arrives to make a final choice. If, however, you already know which names the baby will have, i.e., you're passing down a parent's name, be sure to have this discussion with your wife so it doesn't come as a shock later on.

• Arrange for a deep clean throughout the house in the last few weeks to delivery

About a week or two before the due date, arrange for some good helpers to come and do a final deep clean of the house. Clean the carpets, rugs, move the furniture, dust the light fixtures and fans, make sure bathrooms and cabinets are sanitized. Think of it as spring cleaning except a little more intense because an infant is coming home soon, and these little ones are really sensitive. It's also great to do because mommy and baby will be spending a lot of time on the floor.

Okay, now that we've nailed the essentials, we need to talk about the "birth bag" and the different things you'll need to do depending on your childbirth option.

HOW TO PREPARE FOR A HOSPITAL OR BIRTHING CENTER

There's a lot of paperwork involved when doing either hospital or birthing center, so I encourage you and your wife to go before the due date and take care of any admissions processes that can be done beforehand. That will speed things along once the big day arrives, and the last thing you need is to be stuck with mounts of papers to read and sign when you're wife is screaming in pain. By going early, you also get a chance to scout the facilities. Take a tour of the facility once the pre-registration process is done so you and your wife can get to know the place's layout. Check where the exits and entrances are, the cafeteria for you, and anything else you might need to know. One more important thing you'll need to do is put together a "birth bag." You'll hear that name mentioned quite a bit, and by now, your wife is probably already taking care of it. But since you're an involved and helpful husband, go ahead and double-check with her to ensure she has everything she needs.

The birth bag checklist:

- Toiletries that she likes, e.g., travel shampoo, hairbrush, headband, hair ties, comb, mouthwash, toothbrush/toothpaste, deodorant, soap, and anything else she would like to make her feel presentable and pretty.
- Your ID
- Insurance card and any prefilled hospital paperwork.
- Medications and a medications list if she takes any.
- Her credit card.
- Personal pajamas or special hospital gowns.
- A pair of non-skid socks and some slippers.
- A book or magazine.
- Music playlist or Netflix.
- Cell phone and charger.
- Nursing bra and supportive bra.
- Comfy underwear.
- Pads.
- Going home outfit (think baggy, soft, and comfortable).
- Flip flops.
- Favorite pillow.

- If you know your wife is having a planned cesarean, also consider these items:
- Extra loose clothing.
- Support underwear like special C-section recovery underwear, which is high-waisted and offers light compression.
- Compression wrap like a Belly Bandit for added postpartum belly support.

With a C-section, the new mommy will be away from home much longer than normal delivery, so try as much as possible to get her comfortable and bring her favorite clothes, food, etc.

Most of the basics are generally provided for both mom and baby. So you don't need to worry so much about towels, hospital gowns, disposable mesh underwear, standard pillows, and blankets. The hospitals and birthing centers also provide diapers, hospital branded onesies, standard knit hats, swaddle blankets, pacifiers, shampoo, and in some cases, baby formula. You should call your hospital or birthing center to get full details of what they will offer you. For your new baby, it's likely that you'll only need to bring a few things since the hospital will cover most of the supplies until discharge day. So you and your wife should focus on carrying the going-home outfit, diapers, and wipes, swaddle blankets, mittens, botties, hat, and a blanket if it's chilly. You should also come with the car seat when picking them, and if you're not breastfeeding the child, then a bottle with formula should be at hand.

Don't forget you also deserve a section inside that birth bag since you're going to spend most of the time there, and aside from a little place to crash, there's probably not going to be much for you. **So pack the following:**

- Comfortable clothing to change into pajamas or cozy lounge clothes even if it's a normal delivery.
- Comfortable shoes and perhaps even a pair of slippers.
- Toiletries like shampoo, face wash, toothbrush, and toothpaste.
- Medications if you're on any.
- Glasses or contacts if you wear them.
- Phone and charger so you can send updates to friends and family of the progress and the new arrival. You definitely want to take that selfie when you first hold your baby and go from being a family of two to three.
- Pillow and blanket. I know you're not fancy, but hospital provisions usually suck, so just pack an extra one because you might need it, especially if the labor turns out to be really long.
- Music playlist or a book depending on what

entertains you best. You could use this time to read a book on infants and the first year of life now that you'll be facing that part of the parenting adventure. But you can also just chill, practice some mindfulness and enjoy calming music.

- Favorite snacks and a water bottle. Instead of taking water over a cup, I suggest having a water bottle to ensure you can stay hydrated while on the move.

HOW TO PREPARE FOR A HOME BIRTH

Suppose you've chosen to do a home birth. In that case, your prep work is quite different. First things first, you will need the green light from medical officials that your wife is healthy enough to have a home birth. Only a low-risk pregnancy should be done at home. And even after she receives the green light, you should both continue going for antenatal care until the baby comes. I would encourage you to pre-register with the hospital just in case the home birth doesn't go as planned. Since you have insurance, it doesn't hurt to be pragmatic and prepared. Keep your doctor and midwife in the loop with all these preparations and decisions.

How to prepare your home for the big day:

- Ensure the chosen room is clean with an empty bureau or tabletop.
- The bed should be accessible from both sides and feet.
- There should be a scrub bathtub for use during labor.
- All necessary supplies (your midwife will give you the complete list) should be assembled by week 36 of your wife's pregnancy.
- The room should be well heated for the birth, especially if it's a cold season.
- Make sure the water heater is on and turned up if your wife will use a birth pool. You'll need plenty of heat and hot water during labor and birth.

A checklist for you:

- Take some classes with your wife to prepare for birth and postpartum. You seriously don't want your first visual encounter of childbirth to be in that labor room. At least get some simulated practice what you'll see when the big day finally arrives. Trust me on this. And by the way, if you barf, pass out, and run out of the class during birth, that's okay. Your wife will forgive you.

- Order and shop for all supplies, including linens, by week 36 to ensure both your wife and midwife have everything they need whenever the baby is ready to go.

- Write directions/draw maps for midwives to find your home and, if possible, arrange for a tour before the big day so they can double-check everything is ready. Many midwives are okay with this arrangement, and it avoids the inconvenience of getting lost on D-day.

- Stock up on easy-to-fix foods for labor and postpartum and electrolyte drinks.

- Buy yourself plenty of extra face masks and gloves if needed.

- Make sure there's a phone in the birthing room. Next to it, there should be phone numbers and your home addresses in case emergency calls need to be made. Consider having your local hospital number, your home address, and a few of the people that might need to be contacted in the event of an emergency.

OTHER EXTRAS TO CONSIDER

These recommendations will differ depending on your situation and preference, but I consider it nice to have whether you'll do hospital, birthing center, or home birth.

• **Infant car seat**

I know this is self-evident, but you'd be surprised how many new parents forget or procrastinate till the baby arrives. I have a friend who purchased a baby car seat after the wife gave birth because the nurses told him they would double-check to ensure the infant was riding home in a proper car seat. Frantically, he managed to purchase a good inexpensive one, but it proved challenging to use it when the time came. His lack of practice and nervousness made everything tense and awkward for the new parents even before exciting the hospital doors. Avoid that scenario of having nurses add to your doubts of being a qualified adult and simply buy one early, then make sure they show you how to strap a baby into the car.

• **Frozen dinners**

I recommend cooking about two weeks worth of freezer meals. Consider going for pre-made casseroles and casserole-related dishes as they will become your lifesavers once neighbors, church friends, and relatives stop popping by to bring your dinner or help with the meal preps. You and your wife will not be in the head-space of cooking dinners like before, and you can't rely on take-outs every day, so utilize the last few weeks before delivery to double up on meals. Prepare double your normal portions and freeze the half you don't eat.

THE KEY TAKEAWAY FROM THIS CHAPTER:

- There's no right or wrong way to bring your child into this world. What matters is that you, your wife, and a qualified medical professional agree on the best path to take.
- If your wife is a low-risk pregnancy and you prefer a home birth, make sure you get a midwife that you both feel is highly qualified to take you through that process.
- If you prefer a hospital or birthing center or if your wife is a high-risk pregnancy, then your doctor and hospital caregivers will be with you throughout this experience. You won't have as much freedom as you'd have in-home birth, but it does provide a safer solution for your wife and the new baby. Your insurance is also likely to cover more of the expenses when you use either of these options.

- Regardless of your choice (home birth or hospital), pre-register before the baby arrives and get as much paperwork out of the way. Take a tour of the facilities you'll use and double-check with the nurses regarding the hospital amenities so you can pack the missing extras that you, your wife, and your baby will need during and after delivery.
- Don't forget to help your wife pack a "birth bag" and ensure there's something for you and your newborn as well in that bag. Avoid packing high-value items like Jewelry, loads of cash, and laptops.

Action plan:

It's time to implement everything you learned in the past two chapters. What one thing can you do today to affirm your new status as an expectant dad? Perhaps you can start prepping some frozen meals since you're moving closer to the due date. You can also do a final check of the birthing bag and the baby's nursery to ensure all necessities are stocked up and ready to receive the new bundle of joy.

Go through the checklist given and pick one thing you could do today, even if it means booking a cleaning company to do one final deep cleanse this week.

These last few weeks before delivery will be tough on your wife. Don't forget to be there for her in every way you can. And also, don't forget to give yourself permission to sleep, relax, have a little fun, and practice some self-care because the next phase of your daddy adventure is just about to kick in, and you'll need to be sharp, energetic, and strong for your new family. You've got this.

8

CARING FOR YOUR NEWBORN: ARE YOU UP FOR THE CHALLENGE?

Congratulations dad! This is the part of your adventure where life seems to take on a brighter shade. Regardless of how you got here, what worked and what didn't, the fact is, you and your wife made it. You went from a family of two to three, and now you have a brand new baby boy or girl.

Can you feel that excitement and inexplicable warmth just welling inside you?

You spent the last several months preparing and imagining how life would be like once the baby arrived. No need to imagine anymore. It's time to rise fully into your dad role. There's a living, breathing bundle of joy just waiting on you now and always. The first few weeks and months are pretty disorienting for new parents. Things constantly change, routines seem almost impossible to establish, and you might get to a point where you wonder if your life will ever feel familiar again. When that happens, remember it's something every father had to go through. Although baby's don't come with manuals, there are certain universal principles you can learn to help make the next few weeks a little less chaotic.

If you had a hospital or birth center option, your wife probably spent anything from a few hours to a few days away from home. If it was a home birth and everything went well, then your home has already been filled with the sounds and smells of the new arrival. As you sink into this new reality, you'll need the rest of the material covered in this book to help you get through the first few weeks and months of being a brand new parent. No more rehearsals, daddy, it's go time!

THE BABY'S HERE; WHAT NOW?

You're officially a dad, and there's a new life that now depends on you for protection, survival, and everything in between. As a rookie dad, it's okay to be clumsy, nervous, and at the same time giddy and filled with delight.

NEW DAD | 155

It's a wild ride that first begins with excitement, then settles into endless soiled diapers, crying (lots of crying), and sleep deprivation. No one said it would be easy, but it will be worth it. Some days will be more challenging than others, and that's okay. You have mindfulness tools and techniques to get you through even the most difficult days ahead. Remember, as a new dad, your mission is to care for your baby and your wife. And it's also your mission to form a bond with your new baby.

The first 24 hours after delivery are hectic and a bit of a blur. The mother of your child has been through hell and back. Can you even imagine how much strength and courage it took to go through that delivery? Most men report they feel a tremendous sense of love, respect, and admiration for their wives after going through pregnancy and delivery together. Are you feeling the same way? Good. And while you'll have time in the coming months to show her how much you adore her, it's an excellent time to take the driver's seat on the baby's needs as soon as delivery is over. Your wife will need a few hours to become somewhat normal, so you're probably going to have plenty of time to hold and bond with the baby. If you were invited to cut the umbilical cord, then your introduction already happened. Good for you, daddy!

HANDLING A NEWBORN

If you haven't spent a lot of time around newborns, their fragility can feel intimidating. Don't let your fear of dropping the baby or holding him/her the wrong way stop you from taking the initiative. Just make sure you wash your hands before holding your baby. Newborns don't have strong immunity, so it's easy to infect them. Be very strict about handwashing with everyone who wants to hold the little one.

When holding your baby, cradle the head and make sure you support both the head and neck at all times. While the baby might seem cute enough to shake or throw around, please resist the urge. Shaking an infant can easily cause bleeding in the brain and lead to death. Whether for play or in frustration, don't shake your newborn. If you need to wake your infant, tickle your baby's feet or blow gently on a cheek. No matter what anyone says, your newborn isn't ready for rough play, so don't jiggle them on your knees or throw them in the air.

The first week of the baby's life is extremely fragile, but the good news is that with each week, the baby grows stronger and less vulnerable. Newborns can only do a handful of activities, namely sleeping, eating, pooping, and peeing. Sometimes they make strange noises and movements. You might even notice some irregularities in their breathing, but most of the time, it's nothing to alarm you unless you notice real discomfort, then you should immediately consult a pediatrician. It's okay for a newborn to pause between breaths, breathe rapidly, and then normally for intermittent periods, but the pause should be short.

When the baby cries, they are usually communicating something. "I'm hungry" or "I'm tired" or "I need attention, hold me now," or I have a diaper that's bugging me." You'll learn what your baby's cries are communicating to you with time and practice. When left in charge of feeding time (babies eat a lot!), remember to burp the baby because they tend to swallow air while feeding. A burp always produces a particular sound. You'll also hear a lot of hiccups, sneezes, squeaking, and all kinds of cool sounds from your newborn.

In the first week or so, you'll notice your baby likes to curl up just like they did while in the womb. They might throw out their arms and legs in a startle reflex and curl their toes when you tickle the bottom of their foot. All these movements are pretty standard.

TIPS FOR SURVIVING THE FIRST FEW WEEKS

• Learn the essentials

To be as confident as possible in your new role, be ready to participate in all of the baby's essential activities. That means you need to learn how to change diapers, bathe, burp, and play with the newborn. When the baby cries, you need to be able to soothe him or her back to sleep. You also need to learn how to put the baby to sleep, including the proper sleep positions to ensure the baby doesn't choke or suffocate while sleeping. While you can read about these things, it's kind of like swimming. The best way to learn is to get into the water. In your case, these first few weeks will be your live lessons to sharpen your skills.

• Feeding is a family event

Newborns need a lot of food, which will be the case for a long time to come. So you all need to prioritize feeding the baby. It should be a family event where everyone takes turns, especially if the baby isn't breastfeeding. And even with breastfeeding, four hands are better than two, trust me. Your wife could always use your help, so just ask her what she needs while doing her thing.

Babies feed at least eight times a day, with some taking it as far as 12 times. That means that every two hours, your baby will need to feed. If your baby isn't hungry after two hours, that's okay. Maybe wait another hour or two at most. If your baby is a sleeper, you might find it difficult to keep the newborn awake for a full feeding, and that's where teamwork comes in because as mommy does the feeding, you can "entertain" the baby until it's fully fed. You can also provide comfort and lactation snacks for the new mom. If your baby is on bottles sooner rather than later, come to an agreement with your wife on the times you'll be covering nightshift. Those of us who have done night feeding duty realize what a challenge and a privilege it is. Not only do we help the new mom get some much-needed snooze, but bonding with your newborn in the middle of the night is also a zen-like experience. Hard to explain, so just take my word for it and give it a test drive. One piece of advice, though, if you're going to be the world's best new dad and run night feeding duty, try to keep the lights dim and ensure there's no environmental noise. By this, I mean, don't put loud music or news/Netflix on. Instead, just enjoy the silence together and "be in each other's worlds with minimum interaction. Always remember to burp the baby before putting them down again.

• Think of your baby like a burrito when it comes to swaddling

If observant enough, you'll notice that medical professionals cover the baby up in a particular way known as swaddling, which resembles a wrap with a tiny adorable head sticking out at the top. This is because swaddling is extremely comforting to a newborn. The pressure of the blanket on the baby's body is reminiscent of the womb, and it keeps the newborn from jerking herself awake or scratching herself with hands and fingers. You don't need a special kind of blanket for this (although you could buy one), but you do need a lot of practice. Let your wife help out till you get a handle on it, but it's basically a process that you can break down into the following steps.

First, lay out your blanket on a flat surface and fold it (about 40by40 inches) into a triangle or a diamond shape. Second, fold down the top corner of the blanket. The corner should be on top of the blanket, not underneath. This helps guide your placement of the baby. Your blanket should now resemble the superman symbol with three corners on the sides and bottom and a flat area on top. Third, place the baby on the blanket with the back of the head above the folded top edge. Keep the baby as centered as possible. When the baby is very young (newborn), be very gentle.

Ensure the head and body are properly supported when you do this. Make sure the blanket will not cover the baby's face in any way after you swaddle them. Fourth, place your baby's left arm at their side and gently hold it in place. Alternatively, you can fold the arm across the baby's chest like in the womb but use your instinct on this to see what your baby prefers. Now pull the wrap around the baby's body to the right (your right) side across their body and tuck it under their back on their right side, just below the armpit. The younger the baby, the more snug the blanket should be. It needs to be snugly enough to hold the baby's left arm in place at their side. Lastly, gently place the baby's right arm at their and hold it in place just as you did with the left. The corner of the blanket you folded over will now be trapped between the right side of the baby's body and their right arm. Take the remaining corner and tuck it underneath the baby's body on their left side, ensuring the entire upper body is gently and firmly wrapped with both hands securely in place. The trick here is to ensure you can fit 2 or 3 fingers between the baby's chest and blanket. If it's too tight or too loose, rewrap that baby. All that's left now is to loosely fold up or twist the bottom of the blanket to cover your baby's feet, and you're ready to hold the baby. Great job, dad!

- **OMG - Sleep is everything for both you, mommy, and baby**

The first few weeks and months of the baby will involve a lot of sleep time. A baby under five months typically requires 16 to 20 hours of sleep per 24hours. As much as you want your baby to get in all this sleep, start showing them the difference between day and night because that's not a skill they perfected in the womb. So make sure things are left bright during the day and completely dark, boring, and quiet during the night. After a while, the baby will decide when to spend more time awake and when to sleep.

Another thing you need to know is that newborns are active sleepers. That means they have a fast-paced 20-minute sleep cycle that might have them wiggling and making noise every half hour. So don't get into the habit of picking them up every time they seem to be awake. Give a little time and wait to see if the baby will reorient and snooze again.

When it comes to sleep time, I encourage you to place the baby in its bassinet or crib. Don't get into the habit of lying on the couch with the baby on your chest, no matter how tempting it is. Many infants have died after a fatigued parent has accidentally rolled over their child while sleeping on a couch or after the infant got trapped and suffocated in couch cushions! Yes, they are fragile in that early stage of life. And lastly, both you and your wife should try to sleep as much as possible when the baby's asleep. If you don't have much outside help, use the baby's sleep time wisely because every hour you get some shut-eye helps you stay sane.

• **Don't worry about the stinky poo**

The first month will stretch and test you in every way possible, including how good your gag reflexes are. The first diapers are pretty disturbing for almost every new dad I've talked to. That's because the initial poop you'll experience won't resemble anything you've ever seen. Rest assured that the first black meconium stools are completely normal. As your kid grows into their human role, their diaper will contain a rainbow of colors and textures, particularly over the coming months. But for now, it's okay to see all kinds of spooky stuff on that diaper. The only time to worry is if you're seeing red in the diaper.

BONDING WITH THE NEWBORN

This will be critical for your relationship with your kid and probably deserves a dedicated chapter because bonding for dads won't happen as it does for moms. Although growing evidence shows that dads release hormones similar to that of a new mom, the research indicates this only happens after the birth as the dad actively cares for the newborn. One thing that's bound to happen almost immediately is this enormous sense of responsibility and protection for your kid. And while that's a good thing, don't allow it to overwhelm you to the point that it interferes with your sense of bonding. Spend as much time as you can with your baby to encourage those hormones within you and get you into the mindset of a parent, not just a supporter of your new family.

If your sense of connection with the child feels strained and elusive, consider reaching out to fellow dads for some support. Don't isolate yourself or entertain feelings of guilt. It's perfectly okay if you don't feel as warm and funny like your wife does. Remember, she's had nine months of direct interaction with this kid. You've only just been physically and officially introduced. Work at this as you would any new loving relationship. Many experts advise that dads should consider spending more time with other dads instead of beating themselves up for not feeling that obsessive connection that moms do. Sharing your current experience with other dads can help take the edge off and give you a new perspective which often does the trick.

THE KEY TAKEAWAY FROM THIS CHAPTER:

- Handling a newborn baby requires care, proper hygiene, and a lot of love. The more you practice, the better you'll become.
- The first few weeks will be challenging, but you and your wife can pull through if you prepped things well. The pre-cooked meals, baby zones, and all the other stuff you organize before delivery will enable you to survive the first month of parenthood. Take it one day at a time, be there for each other and focus on progress, not perfection.
- Be extra mindful of feeding times for the baby and help your wife as much as possible with whatever she needs. If the baby is already on a bottle, decide on a feeding shift that works for both of you.
- Bonding with the baby requires conscious effort. If it doesn't come naturally, that's okay. Avoid feeling guilty and seek support from fellow dads so you can ease into this role and activate those bonding hormones naturally. See yourself as a co-parent, not just the man of the house.

Action Plan:

What can you do today to affirm your new status as the best new dad in the world? Consider practicing some of those essential baby care skills that we discussed in this chapter. If the baby is already with you, make an effort to feed, bathe, burp, and put the baby to sleep. If your baby is still on the way, watch a YouTube video or call a fellow dad and ask them what tricks they have for soothing the baby to sleep. Remember, your wife is just as inexperienced as you, so most of these things you'll need to explore, experiment, and learn together. Don't worry about looking silly; it's the action that counts. Practice, practice, and practice some more. That's all your baby needs.

LEAVE A REVIEW - LET OTHER READERS KNOW WHAT YOU THINK

Please share your thoughts on this book with other expectant fathers by leaving a review on the site that you bought it from. If you purchased the book from Amazon, please leave us an honest review on this book's Amazon page.

This is vital so that other potential readers can see and use your unbiased opinion to make purchasing decisions. Taking a few minutes of your time can help more orphaned children worldwide we sponsor from our book selling. Thank you, Dad!

AFTERWORD

When you started this book, you barely felt like a dad, and yet by the time you get to this last part, I have a strong sense that you not only feel better equipped to welcome your new human into the world, you're probably thrilled at the adventure that awaits you. You have an action plan at hand that only requires your dedication and execution. Commit to your new role emotionally, mentally, and physically. Invest time working on your mindset and develop more emotional resilience so you can successfully whither the changes that fatherhood brings. Take steps to secure your short and long-term finances as outlined in the book. The more you feel in control of your finances, the less stressed and overwhelmed you'll be once the baby is born.

We have gone through each of the stages of pregnancy week by week, and you now have a firm grasp and resources that you can come back to if you're ever curious to know what your baby is doing at any given point of the pregnancy. Let this knowledge empower you to support your wife during this time fully. Be thoughtful about when you can surprise her with a little date night and some romance. Look out for signs of her current emotional status and what she can or cannot physically handle. Let her feel that you've got her back no matter what. Take a proactive role with the childbirth options and help her make pragmatic decisions that still meet her ideal wishes. That fine line can be tricky, but together you can figure out which birthing option will serve your family best. Once the baby arrives, it's all hands on deck for you. That's your time to form a connection with the little one and relieve your wife of some of the burden of early child care. The first few weeks are chaotic, and both of you are inexperienced at this, no matter how many baby books you've read. Approach this adventure as a team. Learn, experiment, and do it together, all the while remembering to honor your self-care rituals because only if your cup is full can you show up as the best version of yourself.

The best new dad in the world isn't always going to be perfect. He doesn't have all the answers, and everything doesn't always work according to plan. The best new dad is considered the best because he's invested in his knowledge and has gained as much understanding as possible to be a better version of himself. He is dedicated to his family and is ready and willing to do whatever it takes to create the best outcomes for himself and those he loves. He doesn't resist or shy away from challenges anymore, and difficult situations only prove how strong he has become as a man, a husband, and a father.

That is my hope for you. May this guide empower you in meeting that end, and if you'd like more guidance on how to bond with your newborn and handle your child's first years like a boss, I encourage you to check out my sequel to this pregnancy book. You'll get tips and advice on how to rekindle a romance with your wife, how to find joy in both work and family life, and how to dream bigger so you can give your family the kind of life you feel they deserve to have.

I can't wait to connect with you on the next book and in our Facebook community for new dads. Feel free to shoot me a message sharing what you took away from this book and how it's helped you and your partner enjoy the pregnancy period. I'd also appreciate it if you could leave me a review so that fellow dads can see what you enjoyed most. It also helps me to continue improving my content as I create more books for fellow dads.

Enjoy the journey of dadhood. I'm sure you're going to be great at this!

Ryan Erickson.

FREE GIFT
JUST FOR YOU!

From this free gift, you can find out:

7 mistakes first-time dads make and actionable tips you can apply immediately.

Just visit the link www.ryanericksonbooks.com

RECOMMENDED RESOURCES

Can fetus sense mother's psychological state? Study suggests yes. (n.d.). ScienceDaily. Retrieved November 8, 2021, from https://www.sciencedaily.com/releases/2011/11/111110142352.htm

A Guide for First-Time Parents (for Parents) - Nemours KidsHealth. (n.d.). Nemours Kids Health. Retrieved November 8, 2021, from https://kidshealth.org/en/parents/guide-parents.html

New parents. (n.d.). Pregnancy Birth and Baby. Retrieved November 8, 2021, from https://www.pregnancybirthbaby.org.au/new-parents

Pregnancy & Birth. (n.d.). Parents. Retrieved November 8, 2021, from https://www.parents.com/pregnancy/

N. (2020, June 3). *Tips for First-time Moms on Pre-pregnancy, Pregnancy and Postpartum.* Johns Hopkins All Children's Hospital. Retrieved November 8, 2021, from https://www.hopkinsallchildrens.org/ACH-News/ General-News/Tips-for-First-time-Moms-on-Pre-pregnancy,-Pregnan

Mayo Clinic Guide to a Healthy Pregnancy: 2nd Edition: Fully Revised and Updated: Wick M.D. Ph.D., Dr. Myra J.: 9781893005600: Amazon.com: Books. (n.d.). Mayo Clinic Guide to a Healthy Pregnancy: Second Edition. Retrieved November 8, 2021, from shorturl.at/kmtBI

Made in the USA
Las Vegas, NV
02 February 2022